Wild Science Careers

DINOSAUR SCIENTIST

Careers Digging Up the Past

THOM HOLMES

Enslow Publishers, Inc.
40 Industrial Road
Box 398
Berkeley Heights, NJ 07922
USA
http://www.enslow.com

Library of Congress Cataloging-in-Publication Data

Holmes, Thom.
    Dinosaur scientist : careers digging up the past / by Thom Holmes.
       p. cm. — (Wild science careers)
    Summary: "Explores the science of and careers in paleontology using several
examples of real-life scientists"—Provided by publisher.
    Includes bibliographical references and index.
    ISBN-13: 978-0-7660-3053-4
    ISBN-10: 0-7660-3053-9
    1. Paleontologists—Juvenile literature. 2. Paleontology—Vocational guidance—
Juvenile literature. I. Title.
    QE714.7.H65 2010
    560.23—dc22

                2008019634

Printed in the United States of America

10 9 8 7 6 5 4 3 2 1

To Our Readers: We have done our best to make sure all Internet Addresses in this book
were active and appropriate when we went to press. However, the author and the publisher
have no control over and assume no liability for the material available on those Internet
sites or on other Web sites they may link to. Any comments or suggestions can be sent by
e-mail to comments@enslow.com or to the address on the back cover.

♻ Enslow Publishers, Inc., is committed to printing our books on recycled paper. The
paper in every book contains 10% to 30% post-consumer waste (PCW). The cover board
on the outside of each book contains 100% PCW. Our goal is to do our part to help young
people and the environment too!

Photo Credits: © Albert J. Copley/Visuals Unlimited, p. 111; Associated Press, pp. 47,
83; © Bruce Tepfer/The Academy of Natural Sciences, p. 98; Christian Darkin/Photo
Researchers, Inc., p. 33; Francois Gohier/Photo Researchers, Inc., pp. 24, 85; © Grant
Delin/Corbis, p. 10; James L. Amos/Photo Researchers, Inc., pp. 1, 4; Kalliopi Monoyios,
p. 107; M. Fedonkin, p. 31; © Mike Hettwer, courtesy of Project Exploration, pp. 65, 72, 75,
76; National Geographic/Getty Images, p. 81; Nobumichi Tamura, p. 41; © Paul Sereno,
courtesy of Project Exploration, p. 63; Peter Menzel/Photo Researchers, Inc., pp. 29, 36;
Photo by Thom Holmes, pp. 51, 54, 55, 57; Photo courtesy K. Curry Rogers, p. 91; Science
Faction/Getty Images, p. 8; © Scott Berner/Visuals Unlimited, p. 6; Shutterstock, p. 45;
SPL/Photo Researchers, Inc., p. 13; Ted Daeschler/The Academy of Natural Sciences/
VIREO, pp. 96, 104, 105.

Cover Photo: Science Faction/Getty Images

On the cover: A paleontologist digs for fossils at Flaming Cliffs in Mongolia.

Contents

Introduction

Paleontology is an exciting career that involves many talents. The challenges of finding **fossils** in the wild, the rigors of camping in the wilderness, and the preparation and understanding of fossils are all part of the careers of the leading **paleontologists** described in these pages. The work of a paleontologist is much like that of a detective.

Paleontologists are scientists trained to study the fossils of animals that lived long ago. Instead of solving crimes like a detective does, however, paleontologists solve the mysteries of the distant past by seeking clues in the earth. Using such clues, these detectives not only piece together the bones of extinct creatures but also an idea of how these creatures lived, struggled to survive, and died.

The word *fossil* means "something dug up" in Latin. A fossil is any indication of an organism preserved in the layers of the earth. Any size or kind of organism can become a fossil, from the smallest microorganisms to the largest animals on the planet. All plants and animals on the land or in the sea may become fossilized. But the making of a fossil is a rare event. The creatures that we know about from fossils only represent a tiny fraction of the many millions of organisms that have ever existed.

The most familiar fossils are the bones of **extinct** creatures. These fossils formed when skeletons, shells, teeth, and other hard body parts were preserved by being trapped in mud and sand in layers of the earth. There are also several kinds of fossils produced by other natural processes. These include trace fossils, which provide clues to the presence of

The footprint of a dinosaur is one example of a trace fossil.

ancient organisms. The footprint of a **dinosaur** is one example of a trace fossil. Such footprints were made in the mud and then preserved in rock when the mud dried. Other examples of trace fossils include impressions of skin, feathers, or hair from extinct creatures.

Whatever type they may be, all fossils are windows into prehistoric life. Fossils reveal the many different kinds of life that once existed. They also show that all types of organisms eventually become extinct. Explaining the reasons for extinction is one of the great detective stories of paleontology. In learning about the reasons for extinction, paleontologists come face-to-face with a great detective story that is still being written. By investigating the disappearance of past life, paleontologists also explore the kinds of threats that may affect the future of humans and other creatures in today's world. To learn about the future, one must know something about the past.

CHAPTER 1

Dinosaurs of the Mongolian Desert

"If you're going to find really great fossils, you must go to places where nobody's ever been before," explains paleontologist Mark Norell. "And if nobody's ever been there before, there's usually a reason for it." One such place is Mongolia, a vast, largely uncharted country in Central Asia. The region is remote, there are few roads, and the weather can be extreme. It is not an easy place to bring a team to **dig** dinosaurs.

Mark Norell is an American paleontologist and **curator** of fossils at the renowned American Museum of Natural History (AMNH) in New York. His job is to help collect, organize, study, and care for the museum's vast store of fossils of reptiles, amphibians, and birds. Among these fossils is one of the world's most celebrated collections of dinosaur skeletons. Norell is a dinosaur expert. In any given work year, his schedule is equally divided between expeditions to faraway locations and supervising a staff of fifty scientists and technicians from his office in New York.

Norell has been a part of many fossil-hunting expeditions that were the first to describe spectacular dinosaur discoveries. These include *Mononykus* ("one claw"), a one-meter- (three-foot-) long dinosaur with puzzlingly short arms,[1] the spectacular fossil of a dinosaur sitting on a nest of eggs like a bird,[2] and the remains of fossilized *Oviraptor* embryos (undeveloped baby dinosaurs).[3] He was also part of a team of paleontologists that described two new **species** of small, feathered dinosaurs.[4] All these achievements have a connection to Asia, and it is there that Norell has spent much of his time searching for fossils.

Mark Norell is the curator of fossils at the American Museum of Natural History in New York City.

A Life in Paleontology

Imagine a life that requires you to travel to faraway and remote places every year: to camp in the wilderness, sample foreign cultures, and fight the elements of nature while discovering traces of long-extinct life. Not many people can plan their lives around regularly scheduled trips to the Gobi Desert in Mongolia to search for fossils. Many people might not like making such a difficult trek year after year, but Norell enjoys his work. "I love the desert," he explains. "I've worked in deserts all over the world, and we've found some amazing fossils. Everything from animals sitting on top of their nests' eggs brooding them to embryos in eggs."[5]

When he is not in the desert, Norell works at the museum. The fossil collection of the AMNH is second to none, especially when it comes to dinosaurs. The museum has sponsored many expeditions around the world in search of traces of prehistoric life. Norell counts himself among the fortunate few who have had the privilege of working in this prestigious museum.

The museum's connections to China and Mongolia have given Norell the opportunity to travel to Asia on field expeditions every summer for more than ten years. These travels, among others, have become a part of his annual schedule—which also includes work analyzing the fossils brought back from the field. He often works with many other scientists. It sometimes takes many paleontologists to put their heads together to understand an important new fossil discovery.

The American–Mongolian Dinosaur Connection

The AMNH has a long history of expeditions to Mongolia. Its first large-scale explorations to the area were the Central Asiatic Expeditions of 1922, 1923, and 1925. Their target was the Gobi Desert, a vast wilderness in Mongolia. The museum's leading paleontologist at the time, Henry Fairfield Osborn, believed that fossils of early humans might be found in Mongolia.

Osborn's passion for expedition was shared by another member of the museum staff, Roy Chapman Andrews. Inspired by Osborn's theory that the roots of ancient man could be found in Central Asia, Andrews led some preliminary explorations to Asia in 1916–17 and 1919 before proposing the larger-scale Central Asiatic Expeditions.

Andrews was often seen in the field wearing a broad-brimmed hat and packing a loaded pistol—a likeness borrowed by moviemakers many years later in the creation of the character Indiana Jones.

There is no doubt that Andrews was most at home outside the museum. "I wanted to go everywhere," Andrews wrote. "I would have started on a day's notice for the North Pole or the South, to the jungle or the desert. It made not the slightest difference to me."[6]

Sometimes the most startling discoveries are made in science because of a single person's dedication to an idea. This was to be the case with Andrews. Even though he never found the remains of ancient

Roy Chapman Andrews's dedication to adventure opened doors for future fossil-hunting expeditions to Mongolia. Moviemakers later used his likeness when creating the character Indiana Jones.

humans in the Gobi, he led his team to discover an astounding bounty of dinosaur fossils.

Following the Central Asiatic Expeditions of the 1920s, the world was thrown into political conflict and war. American paleontologists did not have access to Mongolia for sixty years. Scientific teams of Russians, Poles, and Mongolians continued to explore the Gobi with some success during the 1940s, 1960s, and 1970s. Then, in 1990, the AMNH was invited by the Mongolian Academy of Sciences to participate in a joint exploration of the Gobi Desert region. The two institutions have been working together since that time, sending their teams on summer expeditions to the desert's fossil-rich areas. For Norell and his staff, an expedition to Mongolia was the chance of a lifetime. "To us it was a dream come true," remarks Norell. "The Gobi Desert is the Xanadu, the Nirvana, the Valhalla, the Woodstock of paleontological research areas."[7]

The first joint expedition in 1990 was a small affair. Its primary purpose was to familiarize the scientists from both countries with each other and the general areas that they were going to explore. It was a very important step in building trust and friendship among the scientists and their countries that would affect the success of later expeditions.

The first three joint expeditions retraced the steps of the earlier Russian, Polish, and Mongolian teams. Expectations were so high for these expeditions that the size of the crew swelled considerably by the third year. No less than twenty-five Americans—some of whom were journalists, photographers, and television crew members—went along on that trip. The large number of people, particularly those not involved in digging fossils, began to distract from the scientific goals of the expeditions.

Norell and expedition coleader Michael Novacek were disappointed by the results of the third expedition. In 1993 they decided to dramatically scale back the size of the team. "We wanted a summer to ourselves," explained Novacek, "one that allowed us a last-ditch effort to find a fossil treasure trove."[8] The 1993 expedition included only ten Americans—all experienced field workers or scientists—plus their Mongolian colleagues. The expedition needed to be lean and mean if it was going to find fossils in new and unexplored places.

Things went badly at first. Trucks broke down, and one crew member was severely burned on the foot by boiling water from a spilled teapot. But then their luck changed.

After spending a week looking over unspectacular fossils from a familiar location, Norell and the small crew jumped into a couple of trucks and headed off toward some hills on the horizon. Very soon they spotted numerous white fossil remains jutting out of the ground. The crew stopped and everyone fanned out to explore the area. The decision paid off.

"There were literally skeletons lying all over the place," Norell remembered. Many of them were intact and appeared eerily fresh, as if the animals had just recently died. Skeletal fossils are not usually found in such good condition. They are often broken apart, crushed into tiny pieces, and scattered around. But these bones suggested that something sudden and tragic had befallen the victims—preserving them, practically undisturbed, in the middle of their activities.

Norell and his fellow expedition members knew that they had found something special. The small patch of hills—known as Ukhaa Tolgod (OO-kah TOL-gud) to the local people—contained an astounding collection of fossilized dinosaurs, mammals, and lizards. Ukhaa Tolgod has since been described as one of the richest sites in the world in which to find dinosaur fossils.[9]

Fossil Luck

The odds against an animal becoming fossilized are enormous. The odds are lower still that such fossils will remain preserved and protected from wind, rain, and erosion long enough for a paleontologist to discover them one day.

In the case of the dinosaurs of Ukhaa Tolgod, their remains had been protected underground for nearly 80 million years. The fossils were discovered because the ground had weathered away, exposing the fossils where people could find them. The fossils were strikingly white and so well-preserved that many of the skeletons were intact and retained the shape and posture of the animal at the time of its death. The reason for this relates to the climate and landscape in which the animals once lived.

Norell and his colleagues believe that the dinosaurs of the Gobi were probably buried alive by violent sandstorms. Some of them may have been trapped by collapsing walls of wet sand that came tumbling down after a sudden rainstorm. Having been so suddenly buried prevented the bodies of these animals from being torn apart and eaten by other animals.

This accounts for the completeness of many of the skeletons. The sudden death and burial of these dinosaurs often preserved their last act, such as sitting on a nest of eggs, trying to gain shelter from a sandstorm, or the final moments of a life-and-death battle between **predator** and prey.

Norell and his team knew how rare and precious such fossils were. It was important to dig them up as soon as possible. If that was not done, the sun, wind, and blowing sand during just a single season of unprotected exposure could crumble up the fossils and blow them away forever.

Working in the Wilderness

Digging in the desert is hard work. The Gobi Desert is one of the planet's most inaccessible places. Even after more than twelve expeditions to the region, Norell knows that he must always be ready for the unexpected. The Gobi is not a place to explore without a plan. To do so runs the risk of expedition members becoming stranded and lost, putting their lives in jeopardy. There are few maps of the area, so the expedition teams rely on help from Mongolian colleagues to explore the remote territories.

A typical field expedition may last for a month. During that time, the team must take with it everything needed to survive—food, fuel, clothing, tools, and medical supplies.

Most team members sleep in tents using sleeping bags. Norell does not like sleeping bags and, weather permitting, might be found sleeping outside at night. In the case of an emergency, such as a serious injury, it could take days to reach the nearest village. This is the risk that comes with the privilege of hunting for fossils in the Gobi.

There are no medical personnel among the team members. Norell himself is responsible for the team's basic first-aid needs. Although he has some first-aid training, Norell joked that his first-aid kit contains only "aspirin, tequila, and a gun."[10] He is sometimes called upon to bandage minor wounds and help team members get over the kinds of digestive ailments that can happen when exposed to new foods, bad water, and extreme weather.

Daytime temperatures are hot in the Gobi, often about 41 degrees Celsius (105 degrees Fahrenheit) in the sun and even hotter inside the vehicles. Most of the fossil work is done in the blazing sun. Hats, sunglasses, and light clothing make it possible to endure the heat. Good hiking boots are essential because the team spends much of its time on foot scouting for fossils in the areas near the camp. Drinking water is scarce, so the team must bring its own. Water for bathing is even scarcer, and that is unfortunate because working in the Gobi can make for some extremely dirty people. Blowing sand and clouds of dust quickly coat one's clothing, rub into the skin, and powder the hair. Occasionally, the team will come upon a water pool and have a chance to swim and bathe. The time between baths might be one week or more.

A typical expedition will have between five and ten vehicles for hauling people, supplies, and fuel. Some space must also be reserved for hauling back fossil finds. Most of the traveling is done away from paved roads. However, trucks and sand are not a good combination; the team often finds itself fixing engines, changing tires, and trying to keep the vehicles from sinking into the deep sand and occasional mud that they encounter.

Paying attention to the weather is essential for the team's survival. Mongolian weather is often unpredictable. In 1996 Norell and his fellow explorers were suddenly pelted by a downpour of freezing rain and hail that left a flash flood of water up to their knees and over the road. They dared not move the trucks before testing the depth of the water each step along the way so as not to lose any of their precious fossil cargo. In 1998 another mysterious flash flood materialized on a bright, sunny day without a cloud in the sky.[11] Aside from the dangers presented by sudden rain and the constant heat, the team was also on watch for approaching sandstorms for which the Gobi is also famous. Whenever the camp was engulfed by one of these bright orange clouds of sand, the travelers hunkered down for protection and hoped that their trucks and other belongings would be left in place and in good working order.

Another thing expedition members must pay close attention to is food provisions. Norell loves to cook and would often take charge of making meals for the expeditions. He had a significant role in planning what food to bring. During the earlier expeditions, the team stocked up on the usual nonperishable items such as canned meats and dehydrated vegetables. After a few field trips, however, Norell realized that he could just as easily bring along some quality foods, spices, and even wine to make the evening meals more pleasurable for all. It was not unusual for Norell to prepare a meal of sushi rolls stuffed with canned eel; chicken and pasta; or a spread consisting of dried mushrooms, coconut milk, eggplant, onions, and noodles. Obtaining fresh poultry and meat was only possible when the expedition passed through a village. Mongolians are hearty meat eaters and have a particular fondness for lamb, all of the spare parts of which get boiled into stew. Meat goes bad before too long without refrigeration—and expedition teams cannot bring refrigerators with them. But sometimes spoiled meat must be eaten for lack of having anything else. The safest thing to do with bad meat is to fry it up at very high temperatures to disinfect it. On more than one occasion, the team had to cook rancid sheep parts partly infested with maggots and mold. They cut away the bad parts, fried the meat in hot oil, and doused it with shaslik, a coriander-based spice found in Central Asia.[12]

The Fighting Dinosaurs

Despite the hardships of working in the desert, Norell and his team were very successful. This success led to another, unexpected success. Following the Gobi expeditions of the 1990s, the Mongolian Academy allowed Western scientists to examine one of Mongolia's national treasures—a rare and special fossil known as the fighting dinosaurs.

Although the fighting dinosaurs are one of the most famous fossil discoveries from the Gobi

Desert, the fossil was not well-known outside of the Mongolian Academy of Sciences until recently. In 1971 a joint Polish-Mongolian expedition discovered the entwined remains of two dinosaurs, apparently locked in mortal combat. One was the plant-eating *Protoceratops,* the other a small but fierce predator called *Velociraptor.* The skeletons were nearly complete, and it appeared that the two creatures were victims of the sudden collapse of a sand dune that buried them alive, even as they were engaged in a life-and-death struggle of their own.

For many years, the remains of the fighting dinosaurs were only viewable in a dimly lit display in a Mongolian museum. After his successful trips to Mongolia, Norell succeeded in arranging to bring the fossil to America for others to see.

Norell was excited to examine the fighting dinosaurs more closely. "The first—and most remarkable—thing," explained Norell, "is that the two dinosaurs were not just found together, they were touching one another."[13] The *Protoceratops,* a small, horned dinosaur, was crouched and facing its opponent. The *Velociraptor,* lying on its side, was apparently engaged in a vigorous attack. The right forearm of the predator was clamped in the beaklike mouth

The fossils of the fighting dinosaurs are considered a national treasure in Mongolia. The dinosaurs were fossilized caught in a life-and-death struggle.

of the horned dinosaur, as if the plant eater was holding back its attacker. The left forearm of the predator was gripping the neck frill of the horned dinosaur, as if to push itself free. The deadly foot claw of *Velociraptor*, used for making lethal cuts into the flesh of its prey, was embedded in the neck of the *Protoceratops*, "near where the blood supply would flow to and from the head," said Norell.[14]

Not all paleontologists agree that the fighting dinosaurs were in fact fighting at all. There is some controversy concerning whether these dinosaurs were predator and prey or **scavenger** and scavenged. One reason for this is that the *Protoceratops* is less well-preserved than the *Velociraptor,* lacking two **forelimbs**, one hind limb, and the tip of the tail. This suggests that the plant eater may have already been dead by the time that the *Velociraptor* perished—probably in the act of eating it.

However, the popular point of view shared by Norell is that the fighting dinosaurs were indeed caught in the middle of a life-and-death struggle. The fossil is remarkable because it offers a glimpse at the living acts and behavior of the two dinosaurs. It has special significance among the many rarities found in the Gobi Desert.

Living Two Lives

For Mark Norell, life is divided into two exciting parts. One is the thrill of working in some of the most remote and spectacular fossil sites in the world. The other is being a part of the bustling world of science at the American Museum of Natural History. "There are people who know me from the desert," said Norell, "and then there are people who know me here [at the museum]. I have my desert side, and then I have this side. And this side means getting dressed up a couple of times a week for meetings, dinners, cocktail parties, and public openings for new [museum] exhibits."[15] Norell's ability to succeed in the office as well as in the field is his key to success in paleontology.

Norell uses many kinds of knowledge and experience to do his job. It is not only about fossils, he explains: "I like paleontology because . . . it combines lots of different sciences into one thing. For instance there's a lot of biology, there's a lot of geology, there's even things people wouldn't really expect like computer science and engineering in some of the stuff that we do." At one point in his college career, Norell even left paleontology to pursue studies in molecular genetics, the study of inherited traits. This experience has proven to be extremely useful in his fossil work.

Norell became interested in science at an early age. "[I] was always catching animals, having pets, doing experiments, taking apart machines when I was a child. I was always interested in paleontology too, and I started collecting fossils when I was quite young."[16] One way to get involved in science at a young age is to volunteer at a museum. Norell did so at the Los Angeles County Museum, southern California's best-known natural history museum. As a teenager, this volunteer work led to field expeditions to the deserts

MARK NORELL

Occupation: Paleontologist

Title: Curator-in-Charge, Fossil Reptiles, Amphibians, and Birds at the American Museum of Natural History

Specialty: Specimen research; evolution and classification of dinosaurs and fossil birds

Education: Bachelor of Science (BS), Long Beach State University; Master of Science (MS), San Diego State University; Doctorate (PhD), Yale University. Norell's studies focused on biology, paleontology, evolution, and molecular genetics.

of Mexico and California and the opportunity to work side by side with professional scientists. "Basically," explains Norell, "I was doing what I do now."

Norell suggests that students interested in a career in paleontology should study many different subjects. "It's important to get good grades and a well-rounded education [so that you can] get into graduate school. Study hard. There are thousands of bones discovered years ago that still haven't been studied because there are not enough people to do it."[17] Norell says that to become an expert fossil detective, "you have to know something about mathematics, you have to know something about basic biology, but there are lots of other things that are also important. If you do expedition work in foreign countries, it's important to learn how to be good traveler, perhaps to speak a different language." And as Norell's experience in the desert shows, it is very important to "feel comfortable outdoors and under extreme conditions."[18]

CHAPTER 2

Dinosaurs at the Bottom of the World

Patricia Vickers-Rich has discovered some of the toughest dinosaurs that ever lived. They were not the biggest or most ferocious dinosaurs. But these dinosaurs had to be tough because they lived in a part of the world that was once near the South Pole. The polar regions of today's world are the coldest and harshest on the planet. Most kinds of organisms would not survive for long if left to fend for themselves in the Arctic Circle or Antarctica. Earth's polar regions were not always so uninhabitable, however. There is growing evidence that a wide variety of dinosaurs lived within the polar circles. Much of this evidence comes from fossils discovered by Patricia Vickers-Rich and her husband, Thomas Rich, at a site nicknamed "Dinosaur Cove" during the past fifteen years.

Vickers-Rich is a paleontologist and director of the Monash Science Center in Monash, a suburb of Melbourne in southeastern Australia. She is a world-famous paleontologist and geologist. She and her husband—also a paleontologist—have made many important discoveries about dinosaurs and other prehistoric life of Australia.

Vickers-Rich's path to a career in paleontology began in the United States, where she grew up in California. She credits her high school biology teacher for inspiring her to pursue a career in science. Her parents had not gone to college themselves; she was the first in the family to go after a university education. It was big decision for the family—and an expensive one. Vickers-Rich's mother and father

Paleontologist Patricia Vickers-Rich is director of the Monash Science Center in Australia.

were so supportive that they uprooted themselves, sold many of their belongings, and moved with her to California, where she attended the University of California at Berkeley. She studied paleontology and geology there, and later moved to New York to earn advanced degrees from Columbia University.

Vickers-Rich made a connection soon after college that would lead her to Australia. She had a research job in paleontology at the American Museum of Natural History in New York. While there she studied the fossils of birds collected in Australia by joint American and Australian expeditions. This led to a teaching position in the Department of Earth Sciences at Monash University. She also met Australian paleontologist Thomas Rich, whom she married and settled down with in southern Australia. Vickers-Rich has been closely associated with the fossils of Australia ever since.

Down Under Digs

Hunting for dinosaur fossils in Australia is a special challenge. There are few places in the country where **sedimentary rocks** of dinosaur age are found. Many dinosaur fossils of Australia date from the time span known as the Early Cretaceous Epoch, from 145.5 to 99.6 million years ago. At that time, Australia was attached to Antarctica and positioned closer to the South Pole than it is today. Much of it was also covered by a shallow sea. In modern Australia, rocks containing fossils from the days of the dinosaurs are mostly from areas that were once covered by this sea. Because of this, they are mainly fossils of sea creatures. However, fossils of dinosaurs that once lived near the sea are also sometimes found in these rocks. The rocks are often difficult to explore because they

Australia

This drawing shows what the earth was like during the Early Cretaceous Epoch, when Australia was attached to Antarctica. Although much of Australia today is covered by desert, it used to be a polar region.

are still near the ocean. Sometimes these fossil sites can only be reached when the tide is low.

For these reasons, there are fewer dinosaur fossils to find in Australia than there are in other continents such as North America and Asia. When dinosaur bones are found in Australia, the remains have always been incomplete. Nobody has ever found the complete skeleton of a dinosaur in the land down under. Paleontologists who look for dinosaurs in Australia must be especially careful, patient, and persistent to piece together a picture of dinosaur life in their part of the world.

Discovering Australian Dinosaurs

Until the twentieth century, little was known about the dinosaurs of Australia. The first Australian dinosaur fossil to be described was the toe claw of a small carnivore. Only fifty-three millimeters (two inches) long, it was discovered by geologist William Hamilton Ferguson in 1903. He found it near the southern coastal town of Inverloch, in the state of Victoria, while looking for coal deposits. Being a careful scientist, he recorded the precise location of this discovery so that others could explore the same area.[1]

Despite this early excitement over Ferguson's dinosaur claw, no more dinosaur remains were identified in Australia until 1978, when two college students found the ankle bones of a large, predatory dinosaur in the same Inverloch area.[2]

The discovery in 1978 inspired Patricia Vickers-Rich and Thomas Rich to take a closer look at the fossil site documented by Ferguson. While exploring the coastal areas around Inverloch in 1978, they found two additional fossil locations that contained even more fossil bones than those discovered by Ferguson.

In 1979 the couple returned to Ferguson's well-known coastal location, nicknamed "Dinosaur Cove," and began a renewed search for the remains of dinosaurs and other animals that lived in Australia between 105 and 120 million years ago.

Through her connection with Monash University, Vickers-Rich established a volunteer program to recruit helpers to dig the difficult site. Being in the southern hemisphere—the lower half of Earth—the seasons in Australia are the opposite of those in North America. Winter in the United States is summer in Australia. This is because the earth is tilted as it rotates. When a hemisphere is tilted toward the sun, it is summer in that hemisphere. For more than ten years, during the Australian summer months of January, February, and March, a dozen or more volunteers worked with Vickers-Rich and her husband at Dinosaur Cove. Their ability to dig up fossils was greatly affected by the weather and daily schedule of ocean tides.

These paleontologists are excavating at Dinosaur Cove. Dinosaur Cove was the first mine created especially for finding fossils.

Dinosaur Cove's fossil-bearing rocks also posed a challenge for the crew. Although these rock cliffs are out of the water, the rock itself is extremely hard and difficult to penetrate with hand tools. Vickers-Rich's crew often had to use mining equipment, including rock drills and even dynamite, to break open new areas to excavate. As if working a mine, the crew had "to dig many meters underground, following an old stream channel that contained concentrated bones,"[3] Vickers-Rich explained.

Tales of Tides and Dynamite

If you dig for dinosaurs with Patricia Vickers-Rich and Thomas Rich, you are bound to get wet. Another of their favorite fossil locations is found on a stony ocean beach known as Flat Rocks. When the tide goes out each day, it exposes a hole in the rock floor of the beach. Inside the hole, explorers can find a variety of fossils, some of which are those of small dinosaurs. The rock is hard, and the bones are tiny and delicate. Extracting them from the rock takes time and patience. Making the task more difficult is that the hole can only be explored when the tide is low. Otherwise, it is covered with seawater and sand. During the early years of working the site, the fossil hunters waited for the tide to go out and then spent an hour or more emptying it of sand and water. Over time, the team came up with a clever way to make the hole easier to access. Since there is no stopping the incoming tide, the team found a way to secure a tarp over the hole when they were through with the dig each day. The tarp keeps the sand out. Now, when the tide goes out, all they need to do is remove the tarp, pump the water out of the hole, and sweep it clean with brooms to expose the surfaces where fossils are found. With the hard work of a team of dedicated volunteers, what once was only a small hole in the rocky beach has been gradually broadened so that several people can work inside it at the same time. Workers also scout the surrounding area regularly for additional patches of fossils that wear out of the rock from time to time.

Many hundreds of small fossil bones are found at Dinosaur Cove and Flat Rocks each season. They include back bones and leg parts of large predators, bony plates from the backs of armored dinosaurs, teeth, parts of skulls, dinosaur footprints, and other small bone pieces. In 2008 alone, more than seven hundred fossil bones and teeth were recovered at these sites. Among the most spectacular discoveries were the upper jaw and several limb bones of small, plant-eating dinosaurs; at least twenty-eight individual teeth from plant-eating dinosaurs; and six teeth from carnivorous dinosaurs.

The most common dinosaur remains found at the Dinosaur Cove are those of small, chicken-sized, plant-eating dinosaurs that walked on two legs. One skull of this chicken-sized dinosaur provided enough evidence to name a new kind of dinosaur. Vickers-Rich and her husband named it *Leaellynasaura* after their daughter, Leaellyn.

THE DRIFTING CONTINENTS

The story of Australian dinosaurs is, in part, the story of the changing face of Earth's landmasses. If you look closely at a world map, you can see that the outlines of certain continents seem to match up like the pieces of a jigsaw puzzle. It is obvious that the east coasts of North and South America closely match the west coasts of Europe and Africa. When put together, they appear to have been a part of a single landmass that must have broken apart. Scientists agree that this is what happened. But how could this be possible?

Ever since Earth's formation, the outer surface, or crust, has been moving. The crust is made up of a dozen or more large slabs called tectonic plates. What causes the plates to move is the underlying layer, called the mantle, on which they rest. The mantle is heated by Earth's core, which creates thick, molten magma. The hottest magma rises through the mantle, comes in contact with the underside of the crust, and then slowly falls again as it cools. This rising and falling moves the tectonic plates. The movement of these plates results in continental drift, the slow shifting of the positions of the continents. The movement is slight—only about five centimeters (two inches) per year. Over long periods of time, this can dramatically change the planet's surface.

The continent of Australia is currently an island. But it was at one time connected to a giant landmass that also contained the other continents. Life evolved on this single landmass and then became isolated as the landmasses separated over many millions of years. Because of this, animals found on Australia evolved without contact or breeding with animals on other continents, slowly changing them into the unique creatures that we still see there today.

But dinosaurs are not the only fossilized creatures found in the Dinosaur Cove area. The site has recently become famous for the remains of several small mammal jaws. These important fossils were found by volunteer helpers at the site. Information from these jaws can tell paleontologists much about the kinds of mammals that lived at the same time as the dinosaurs in Australia.

Drawing Conclusions About the Lives of Polar Dinosaurs

The southern polar region familiar to the creatures of Dinosaur Cove was not the snow-covered ice sheet that comes to mind when most people think of the South Pole. In fact, the temperature may never have dipped below freezing. But with an average yearly temperature of about 10 degrees Celsius (50 degrees Fahrenheit), it was not warm, either.

"In this cold place," explained Vickers-Rich, "the sun did not shine for three months during the winter."[4] How did the little dinosaurs found at Flat Rocks and Dinosaur Cove survive this dark winter? Evidence from the microscopic study of their bones suggests that these dinosaurs grew steadily all year long. This means that they did not hide away to hibernate for the winter, but remained active throughout the cold season. Evidence from their skulls shows that they had large, well-developed eyes. Having such good vision would have enabled these dinosaurs to see in the dark of the polar winter. Vickers-Rich suggests that some small dinosaurs may have even burrowed into the ground to protect themselves against the chill of the long winter nights.

The idea that dinosaurs could have lived in such cool regions of the earth was virtually unthinkable fifty years ago due to the widespread belief that dinosaur biology was like that of modern reptiles.

Leaellynasaura

The existence of these dinosaurs in such a cold place suggests that some dinosaurs were active and energetic like today's birds and mammals. This contrasts an old view that dinosaurs were sluggish and cold-blooded like today's reptiles. Being warm-blooded would have allowed the dinosaurs to maintain a steady body temperature even without heat from the sun. It is also possible that these small creatures of the far south had feathers on their bodies to provide insulation from the cold.

Because of the efforts of Patricia Vickers-Rich and Thomas Rich, there has been growing interest in finding more clues to the fossil past of Australia. Their work has added immensely to the history of prehistoric life from that part of the world.

The Life of a Paleontologist

Vickers-Rich's love of paleontology goes beyond the discovery of fossils. Like many paleontologists, Vickers-Rich's job takes her to many interesting parts of the world. "Because I am a fossil hunter," says Vickers-Rich, "I go to many remote places: the steppes of Tatarstan [in Eastern Europe], the deserts of Patagonia, the rain forests of Sri Lanka, the dinosaur-bearing beds of Zigong, China, and the plateaus of Wyoming. I love going to such places, for they are

PATRICIA VICKERS-RICH

Occupation: Paleontologist and Geologist

Title: Director of the Monash Research Centre, Monash University

Specialty: Prehistoric environments, ecosystems, and the evolution of organisms including dinosaurs and birds

Education: Bachelor of Arts (BA) in paleontology, University of Berkeley; Master of Arts (MA) in geology, Columbia University; Doctor of Philosophy (PhD), Columbia University

wild, wonderful, and hold many secrets that I hope I will unlock for the first time."[5]

Being a paleontologist has given her a glimpse of many different places and cultures. "My discoveries occur every day—and are not only about fossils," reveals Vickers-Rich. "When I go to an area, I am just as interested in the people, the trees, the animals, the politics, the languages spoken, or the jokes told, as I am [in] the fossils."[6]

Of course, not all of her time is spent in the field. Days in the office may seem boring to others, but for Vickers-Rich every day is one of discovery. This is part of being both a teacher and a scientist. An expert such as Vickers-Rich is in great demand by others who want to learn about fossils. "I spend time with local school kids, give radio interviews, and work on TV documentaries," she explains. "I also spend time raising funds for research and the Monash Science Centre."[7] After all of that, she also finds time to teach college classes about geology and fossils—and to walk her dog!

Vickers-Rich believes that where there is a will to accomplish something, there is a way to make it happen. This kind of attitude is important to have in a science like paleontology. Her advice to students who want to pursue a career in paleontology is to keep a positive—and realistic—outlook. "If you want to be a paleontologist," says Vickers-Rich, "don't let people discourage you—but don't think you are going to make a lot of money doing it. Follow your dreams."[8]

CHAPTER 3

Giant Dinosaurs From Argentina

There are no trees in Patagonia. That is the first thing one notices about the vast badlands of Argentina. The earth is parched, and the sparse plants barely cover the ground. "Argentina is a good place for finding fossils, especially because of Patagonia," explains paleontologist Rodolfo Coria.

Patagonia makes up about 50 percent of the surface area of Argentina. The rocks are "very well exposed," says Coria, "so it's very easy to find fossil evidence. If you're looking for dinosaurs, Patagonia is the place."[1]

Rodolfo Coria is a skilled paleontologist who finds himself in the middle of an extraordinary period of dinosaur science in his native land of Argentina. New discoveries often bring paleontologists from other countries knocking on Coria's door. In addition to his fieldwork, Coria is director of the Carmen Funes Municipal Museum in Plaza Huincul. He is based in Neuquén Province, a thinly populated area in western Argentina, in the northwestern corner of the Patagonian badlands. The museum proudly displays life-size skeletal reconstructions of *Argentinosaurus* and *Giganotosaurus,* two giants that once roamed Patagonia—and that Coria helped discover.

An Unexpected Beginning in Paleontology

Coria grew up in Buenos Aires, Argentina. An early love of science led him to an interest in animals and their biology. After high school, Coria enrolled in veterinary school. He quickly realized, however, that

Rodolfo Coria stands next to the skull of *Giganotosaurus*, one of the dinosaurs he helped discover.

he was less interested in taking care of sick animals than in understanding how they worked. Coria's real interest was in comparative anatomy—studying the ways that different animals are put together. After leaving veterinary school he decided to become a science teacher and went to teacher's college.

Coria had an eye for bones and was a gifted artist who could make detailed and accurate sketches of animals and bones. In anatomy class, Coria played a bone guessing game with his friends: "We would form partners, and one partner would toss a bone across the room to the other, and the second partner had to identify the bone before he caught it."[2]

Coria did not finish teacher's college. He was instead sidetracked into a career in paleontology. While still a student, he volunteered for a job at the Buenos Aires Museum of Natural History. He worked for José Bonaparte, whose legendary fossil discoveries number in the dozens. Coria recognized this as a great opportunity and worked hard to please the most famous paleontologist in his country. Because of his work with Bonaparte, Coria began to see that there might be a way of making a living with his skill in anatomy. He helped Bonaparte by preparing fossils for examination and sketching pictures of them for publication in scientific papers.

Coria's big break came in 1985 with the discovery of a magnificently odd meat-eating dinosaur in Argentina. Bonaparte called it *Carnotaurus*—the "bull lizard"—after two stumpy horns on its brow. It was three meters (ten feet) tall at the hips and up to nine meters (thirty feet) long, making it one of the largest predators discovered in South America by that time. Bonaparte not only asked Coria to draw the technical illustrations for the scientific report on *Carnotaurus,* he also asked Coria to coauthor the scientific paper

A HISTORY OF FOSSIL DISCOVERIES

Dinosaur discoveries are not new to Argentina. The country has been the location of many unusual fossil finds over the past hundred years. The dinosaurs found in Argentina have a history of breaking records. Argentina is currently the home of the oldest known dinosaurs (*Eoraptor* and *Herrerasaurus*), the largest meat-eating dinosaur (*Giganotosaurus*, "giant southern lizard"), and the biggest and bulkiest plant-eating dinosaur (*Argentinosaurus*, "Argentina lizard"). If these distinctions were not enough, a discovery in 1999 by a joint team from the United States and Argentina has uncovered a rare and remarkable fossil location: a vast dinosaur nesting ground where huge, long-necked plant eaters once laid thousands of eggs.

with him. This gesture of Bonaparte's put Coria in the limelight of dinosaur discovery and set him on a firm career path as a paleontologist. With this accomplishment, at the age of only twenty-three, Coria was offered a full-time job at the museum.[3]

Coria worked in Buenos Aires for four years until he was offered a job as chief paleontologist and museum director in the small town of Plaza Huincul on the edge of the Patagonian badlands. Coria made a name for himself in Plaza Huincul with the discovery of large dinosaurs in the vicinity.

The Biggest of the Big

In 1988, a farmer in Neuquén province led Bonaparte and Coria to a bone in the ground that turned out to be an amazing discovery. After months of digging, Bonaparte's team found several bones of a huge, long-necked, plant-eating dinosaur. One of the back bones, or **vertebrae**, was more than one-and-a-half meters (five feet) tall, the largest of any known dinosaur. Although only about 10 percent of the animal was found, there was enough evidence for Bonaparte to compare this new specimen to other similar dinosaurs. Coria helped Bonaparte prepare the bones for study and also made the scientific illustrations of the skeleton. In 1993 Bonaparte and Coria published their description of the plant-eating dinosaur, which they called *Argentinosaurus*. It is still considered the heaviest, or bulkiest, dinosaur known.

In the study of dinosaurs, finding a plant eater is sometimes only half of the quest. For every plant eater there surely must have been a meat-eating dinosaur of one kind or another hoping to make a meal of it. As Coria knows so well, the world of dinosaurs contained both kinds of creatures. In Patagonia, scientists often find both parts of the puzzle. "Big preys and big predators," as Coria explained.

Finding a Big Predator

The first bones of *Giganotosaurus* were found in the badlands not far from a roadside near Plaza Huincul. Although it lived after the time of *Argentinosaurus,* the specimen of *Giganotosaurus* provided the first local clues to the kinds of predators that could have attacked such large plant eaters. *Giganotosaurus* was described in 1995 by Coria and his colleague Leonardo Salgado, who immediately recognized it as one of the largest predatory dinosaurs ever discovered. Fossils from Patagonia are rarely complete

Giganotosaurus is one of the largest predatory dinosaurs ever discovered.

skeletons, and they are often dry and cracking when they are taken out of the rock. By these measures, the specimen of *Giganotosaurus* was quite complete. The original specimen included about 70 percent of the bones. They revealed a large predator measuring about twelve meters (forty feet) long. In 1998 Coria and another colleague announced the discovery of a new specimen of *Giganotosaurus* consisting of an even larger lower jaw. The size of this jaw showed that *Giganotosaurus* could have grown to be about fourteen meters (forty-six feet) long.

Giganotosaurus had a large, long skull with a bony ridge running along each side of the snout and low, rounded brow horns just before the eyes. Its jaw was lined with slender, bladelike teeth, the longest of which were about fifteen centimeters (six inches) long. Unlike tyrannosaurs, whose teeth were shaped like bananas and could crunch the bones of their prey, the jaws and teeth of *Giganotosaurus* were well-adapted for ripping ribbons of flesh from their prey, probably while gripping them with their large hand claws.

Even after the discovery of *Giganotosaurus*, there were more exciting predatory dinosaurs to be discovered in Argentina. In 1997 another visit with a local farmer led Coria to a fossil site about a half hour's drive from Plaza Huincul. Canadian paleontologist Philip Currie was visiting Coria at the time. After checking out the fossils the farmer had found, Coria and Currie made a chance discovery while traveling through the area. "We were very lucky because looking in the slope of this hill we found this bone," explained Coria.[4]

The bone turned out to be that of another large meat-eating dinosaur. Coria and Currie established the Argentinean-Canadian Dinosaur Project to dig up the fossil. After the first field season, which lasted several weeks, they realized that the site contained more than one skeleton. It took five field seasons from 1997 to 2001 to complete the excavation.

Searching for *Mapusaurus*

The excavation of the site was an enormous undertaking. This was due in part to having many individual specimens to extract from the rock, but it was also because the dinosaurs themselves were so large. Extracting the fossils required five years of hard work in weather conditions that were often challenging.

Whereas February and March are often snowy and cold in the northern hemisphere, these months mark the end of the hot summer in South America.

The days of late summer are still hot, often close to 38 degrees Celsius (100 degrees Fahrenheit). But at night the temperature may dip below freezing. Digging up dinosaur fossils in Patagonia requires camping in the wilderness. Scientists must be prepared for the hot and the cold. Dinner is cooked late and eaten around a campfire. Water is used sparingly, mostly only for drinking. Everyone goes to sleep soon after dinner in a cozy sleeping bag to conserve energy for the next day's work.

Coria and his team cooked their meals over a campfire.

These are some of the hand tools Coria and his team used to dig for fossils.

An enormous amount of work is required to dig out such an enormous number of bones. The first week was spent chipping away with shovels, picks, chisels, and hammers at the massive amount of rock, called **overburden,** that covered most of the site. The crew removed an estimated fourteen to eighteen metric tons (fifteen to twenty tons) of rock over the course of a week—enough to fill a few small trucks. All of this was done using only hand tools and plastic buckets to carry the rock to a waste pile.

Heavy rains set in after a few days, making the experience even more demanding. The camp was separated from the fossil site by a steep gorge about six meters (twenty feet) deep. When it rained, the whole site became covered with water and mud. The crew crossed the gorge each day to get to the fossil site, hugging its muddy sides so as not to slip or fall. At night, mud and water seeped up from the ground inside the tents, making it a challenge to stay dry. Currie and Coria directed the crew to rig a tarp over the dig site to protect it—and themselves—from the driving rain that lasted for several days without end.

When it was not raining, the sun beat down on the crew without mercy. Finding a shady place to rest was a challenge. Without any trees, crew members often found themselves huddling behind a rock wall or in their hot tents, where the sun could not beat down on them directly. Sun exposure is sometimes more intense in that part of the world than in North America due to the thinner ozone layer that normally protects the surface of the earth from harmful ultraviolet rays. With less protection, crew members become more susceptible to sunburn. Wearing protective clothing and sunscreen was important. A hat with a flap for covering the back of the neck was also handy.

Despite the challenges, the team recovered at least seven individual fossils of different sizes from the same bone bed. The specimens ranged in size from

The camp's tents came in handy for hiding from both rain and the hot sun.

five to twelve meters (seventeen to forty-one feet), making them among the largest meat eaters known.

Coria and Currie named the new dinosaur *Mapusaurus* ("earth lizard"). Its immense size rivaled that of its close relative *Giganotosaurus.* The skull of *Mapusaurus* differed significantly from that of *Giganotosaurus* by having a shorter snout, narrower shape, and a bumpy ridge extending on each side of the skull from just behind the nostril, over the brow, and behind the eye. The teeth of *Mapusaurus* were as knifelike as those of *Giganotosaurus.* This fact is possibly connected to its prey—large plant eaters such as *Argentinosaurus.*

DISCOVERING DINOSAUR EGGS

In 1997 Rodolfo Coria was joined by a small expedition from the Los Angeles County Museum to explore a remote corner of northwestern Patagonia. This team set out hoping to find fossil bird remains. Instead, on only their second day in the field, they stumbled upon something entirely different. Driving through the badlands, they spotted a promising rock face in the distance. The area is mostly flat but distinguished by highly eroded rock flats that rise above the plains like gigantic sand castles. Having gone as far as they could go in their truck, the paleontologists stopped and began to walk in the direction of the rock face. Before they got very far, however, they began to notice something strewn over the ground. There were fossil fragments all around them. Step by step, they were all beginning to find fossilized chunks of dinosaur eggs. Paleontologist Luis Chiappe, of the Los Angeles County Museum, recalled, "We realized that the entire place was virtually paved with these eggs and fragments of eggs. The concentration of eggs was so intense and rich that, in an area of roughly 91 by 182 meters (100 yards by 200 yards), we counted about 195 clusters of eggs."[5]

Each cluster contained a half dozen or more eggs. Each egg was only about twelve to fifteen centimeters (five to six inches) in diameter and nearly round. The scientists soon realized that they were walking through a vast nesting site of some kind of dinosaur. Dinosaur eggs are one of the rarest fossil discoveries, yet here the paleontologists were, surrounded by thousands of them. It was the discovery of a lifetime.

During the first short field season, they recovered several excellent egg specimens. Expedition members from the Los Angeles County Museum returned to the United States to examine them in a laboratory. In early 1998 Marilyn Fox, an expert at

AND EMBRYOS IN ARGENTINA

preparing fossil specimens, was carefully chipping inside one of the fossils when she discovered something extraordinary—tiny bones. The egg contained the fossilized remains of an unhatched dinosaur embryo. She hoped that enough of the tiny creature was intact so that it might reveal what kind of dinosaur had laid the egg. After weeks of slow and painstaking preparation, it became clear that the tiny dinosaur embryo belonged to a family of some of the largest dinosaurs—the long-necked, plant-eating titanosaurs. This was a smaller kind of dinosaur from the same group that included *Argentinosaurus*.

The team even recovered fossilized skin—impressions of dinosaur skin—the first for any variety of unhatched dinosaur egg. The fossil pattern clearly showed the reptilian scales that made up the dinosaur's skin. Each embryonic titanosaur measured about thirty centimeters (twelve inches) long inside the egg.[6] That is an amazingly small size for a dinosaur that might one day have been eighteen meters (sixty feet) long.

The expedition team returned to the site for three more years. Each time, Coria, Chiappe, and others found more eggs and other surprises. The paleontologists discovered at least four layers of egg sites on different geologic levels, each of which was laid at a separate time. This told the scientists that the same nesting site had been used repeatedly, possibly for many breeding seasons in a row.

The magnitude of the Patagonian egg site is so extensive that Coria believes it will take many years to fully explore. He called the site "unique," a once-in-a-lifetime opportunity to study the entire **ecosystem** of these dinosaurs. The area includes not only fossils of the titanosaurs and their eggs, but of ancient plant life and other creatures, including other dinosaurs, that lived in the same area with them.[7]

RODOLFO CORIA

Occupation: Paleontologist and Museum Director

Title: Director of Carmen Funes Municipal Museum

Specialty: South American dinosaurs and their evolution

Education: Doctorate (PhD) in paleontology from the University of Argentina, Buenos Aires

Hard Work Pays Off

"The teeth of the new animal [*Mapusaurus*] are better adapted for going after really big dinosaurs," explained Currie, "like the long-necked plant eaters that lived in that region. If you look at the teeth, they are very bladelike; they have serrations running down the front and the back and the teeth themselves are very narrow and knifelike."[8] These teeth would have made it easier for *Mapusaurus* to attack an animal that was much larger than itself. If *Mapusaurus* used its teeth to rip strips of flesh from the side of *Argentinosaurus,* the giant plant eater would bleed severely, weaken, and eventually collapse.

The *Mapusaurus* fossil site was unique because it contained many individual dinosaurs. They ranged in size from juveniles to adults. At the time the dinosaurs lived, the area was affected by torrential flooding, probably from seasonally heavy rains. Coria cannot tell for sure if the dinosaurs died over the course of many years or all at once. One theory suggests that they were traveling in a group and were overcome by a violent rush of floodwater.

Evidence that large kinds of predatory dinosaurs traveled in groups is extremely rare. The remains of most predatory dinosaurs are found by themselves. It is generally assumed that they hunted alone. If these fossils of *Mapusaurus* represent a group that was traveling together, it might mean that these dinosaurs hunted in packs. If this were the case, perhaps they worked together to bring down such gigantic prey as *Argentinosaurus.*

To paleontologists like Coria and Currie, such evidence provides a special look into the behavior of these extinct animals. Currie said, "It seems to me that we have very convincing evidence that large meat-eating dinosaurs formed these social groups where the young and the old worked together, hunted together, and lived together."[9]

Coria agrees that the dig provides evidence that *Mapusaurus* lived and traveled in groups. He notes that the site only contained fossils of this one kind of animal. If the fossil bed had been created by a more random process—such as a bend in a river that once collected the stray bones of many different animals that died upstream—one would expect it to include remains of other kinds of animals as well. Instead, the evidence strongly suggests that these animals were together before they died because of a localized natural disaster, such as a flash flood.[10]

Paradise for Paleontologists

The Patagonian badlands of Argentina remain one of the most remote and exciting frontiers of dinosaur science. In Patagonia, most new dinosaur discoveries are different from dinosaurs discovered there before. It is paradise for a paleontologist like Rodolfo Coria. If he keeps up the great work, we will be hearing much more about his amazing discoveries for years to come.

CHAPTER 4

Lost Dinosaurs of Africa

If you like to travel to exotic places, then you might like the field of paleontology. As glamorous as this may sound, however, do not expect to find the comforts of home while working in the field. Much fieldwork is done in harsh places that are often too wet, too hot, too dry, too cold, or some of each.

Going on a field expedition usually requires hard physical work in remote locations where water and food are scarce and where you sleep the best you can in a tent or under the stars.

Paul Sereno is one of the most well-traveled paleontologists, even in a field where travel is often required of the work. Although he also teaches at the University of Chicago, he seems most at home in the wilds of some far-off land, hunting for new dinosaur fossils. His expeditions have often taken him to rarely explored regions of the southern hemisphere, including South America and Africa. Since finishing graduate school in 1987, Sereno has led expeditions to Argentina three times, Niger four times, and once each to Morocco, Brazil, Australia, India, and Inner Mongolia. He has worked on a wide range of fossil creatures from the Mesozoic Era, the time of the dinosaurs that lasted about 180 million years. He has discovered and described the world's largest crocodile specimen, the earliest meat-eating dinosaur, a bizarre plant-eating dinosaur with six hundred teeth, a meat-eating dinosaur that could have been longer than *Tyrannosaurus rex,* a giant predatory dinosaur with a head like a crocodile's, and a long-necked,

Paul Sereno has led paleontological expeditions to many different countries, including some rarely explored regions. In this photo he is dusting off a piece of skull during his 2000 expedition to Niger.

plant-eating dinosaur measuring twenty-one meters (seventy feet) long.

Sereno's finds in Africa have told us much about the mysterious creatures that lived in the southern hemisphere when the age of the dinosaurs was coming to a close. Much is known about North American and Asian dinosaurs that lived at that time, but much less was known of their cousins on the other side of the world. It was a time when the land bridges that once connected the northern and southern hemispheres were breaking apart, leaving dinosaurs from the north and south to evolve in different ways. Their different environments caused these geographically separated creatures to adapt to their local worlds. The discovery of the African plant eater *Jobaria,* for example, showed that some kinds of long-necked, plant-eating giants still lived much as their ancestors had, even after these same kinds of dinosaurs had become extinct in North America.

In the history of modern paleontology, Sereno must be considered a champion dinosaur hunter. Working from his base at the University of Chicago, this American scientist has had a tremendous knack for diving into challenging expeditions and coming away with startling new discoveries.

The Making of a Paleontologist

Sereno is now one of the world's most accomplished paleontologists, but when he was young nobody expected much of him. After nearly failing the sixth grade, young Paul just did not show the same level of interest in school as his five siblings. What got him through middle school and high school was his interest in art and drawing. But he still had no solid plan for his life, even after graduating from Northern Illinois University.

Sereno's decision to study paleontology came after he visited his brother in New York—who at the time was studying geology and fossil science. While in New York, Paul took a behind-the-scenes tour of the American Museum of Natural History. He was able to get an up-close look at the museum's enormous collection of dinosaur fossils. Sereno later said, "I never recovered from that visit."

Sereno decided to go to graduate school at Columbia University to study paleontology. He soon learned that his chosen field would be a great way to combine his interest in art, travel, science, and geology.[1] After getting his graduate degrees, Sereno returned to Illinois in 1987 and began teaching at the University of Chicago. He led his first expedition to South America in 1988 to search for some of the earliest known dinosaurs. His success in South America led to an amazing series of expeditions during the 1990s, primarily to Africa, and the discovery of many new, unknown dinosaurs.

Dinosaurs of the African Desert

Sereno's first dinosaur-hunting trips were to South America, where he successfully searched for evidence of the earliest known dinosaurs. Being acquainted with dinosaurs of the southern continents, he was fascinated by how different they were from those of North America and Europe. This led Sereno to continue his search for dinosaurs in other lands below the equator. One such place was the country of Niger, in northern Africa. The Sahara Desert makes up much of Niger, where nomadic people live in sparsely populated areas. The desert is also known for having rock formations dating from the Cretaceous Period, the last great span of time during which dinosaurs lived.

"We really know very little about the kinds of dinosaurs that lived in Africa during the Cretaceous, the last period of the dinosaur era," explained Sereno. "Almost all of the evidence [from] this time comes from North America and Asia."[2] Sereno was hoping to find new fossils that would fill some gaps in the history of dinosaurs below the equator—a time when Africa was geographically isolated from the north.

Sereno's first opportunity to visit Niger came in 1990. He tagged along with a British expedition that was searching for fossil fish. The first trip lasted two months, but only ten of those days were spent looking for fossils. Most of the time was spent traveling by Jeep and ferry from London to Niger. Driving four vehicles, the expedition crossed the English Channel by ferry and sped across France. From there they caught another ferry across the Mediterranean Sea to reach Tunisia in northern Africa. From Tunisia they drove the rest of the way to Niger. They had a location in mind based on the expeditions of previous explorers. Pinpointing the fossil location in the Sahara was also a challenge. "We used compass bearings and maps," said Sereno, "because the global-positioning-system of satellite navigation was not yet operative in the Sahara."[3]

Working with a local Tuareg chieftain, Sereno discovered a graveyard of bones from long-necked, plant-eating dinosaurs. There was little time during that expedition to do more than make note of the location of the bones. "Someday, I would return," Sereno vowed to himself.[4]

During expeditions to Niger in 1993 and 1997 and Morocco in 1995, Sereno's team made several startling discoveries: a new ten-meter (thirty-foot) predatory dinosaur that they named *Afrovenator* ("African hunter"), an even larger predator called *Deltadromeus* ("agile river runner"), and an exquisite skull of one of the largest meat eaters ever found: *Carcharodontosaurus* ("shark-toothed lizard"). Sereno's newly found skull of *Carcharodontosaurus* could have once been attached to a body that was more than eleven meters (thirty-seven feet) long, ranking it among the world's largest known predatory dinosaurs. Other astounding finds included an eleven-meter (thirty-six-foot) specimen of *Suchomimus* ("crocodile mimic"), a peculiar fish-eating predator with a long snout like a crocodile, and the twenty-one-meter (seventy-foot) plant eater *Jobaria*, named for Jobar, a mythical creature from the lore of North African nomads.

The Biggest Expedition

After having already made three trips to Africa, Sereno mounted his largest expedition ever in 2000. He used what he had learned about traveling quickly and efficiently to Niger to maximize his time in the field. Sereno's 2000 expedition team consisted of fourteen people: students, professional paleontologists, and fossil-hunting enthusiasts. The entire trip lasted for 116 days, 96 of which were spent in the field digging for dinosaurs and other fossils. The super-efficient team even maintained a Web site from the field so that interested visitors could learn about daily discoveries, read messages from team members, or even see what was on the team's menu for dinner.

Although having a Web site was considered to be innovative in 2000, the computer age could do nothing to make the backbreaking work of digging fossils any easier. In the desolate, sand-covered regions of the Sahara Desert, Sereno's team used many of the same techniques for finding and digging fossils that had been perfected by other scientists decades before. To make the best use of the expedition's time, Sereno met with the team at 6:45 A.M. daily to go over the plans for the day. During their first days in the field, the team carefully walked the fossil-bearing areas looking for specimens and then set about the painstaking task of digging them up. Several dig camps were set up, and the team was divided so that more than one site could be dug at the same time.

Living in the desert for four months was often difficult. Occasional sandstorms interrupted the team's work. Sixty-four kilometer-per-hour (forty mile-per-hour) winds would have blown their tents over if they had not properly fastened them to the ground with stakes. Temperatures from day to night in the desert often fluctuated wildly by 27 degrees Celsius (80 degrees Fahrenheit). One of the hottest temperature readings was higher than 49 degrees Celsius (120 degrees Fahrenheit). The team brought along five kilograms (ten pounds) of sunscreen to protect themselves from the sun. They lived on canned and packaged foods because no refrigeration was

In the field, Sereno holds a team meeting every morning to brief the team on the dig plans for the day.

available. Items on the menu often included freeze-dried chunks of chicken and powdered milk and cheese. The team hauled more than 394 liters (104 gallons) of diesel fuel with them for their vehicles. Of course, the desert had no bathrooms, so the toilet consisted of "a shovel, toilet paper, and the nearest dune."[5]

After several weeks of exploring, the work paid off in spectacular ways. A picture of Africa as it must have been about 110 million years ago began to emerge. The sand and stone yielded a wealth of fossil animals and even evidence of plants, suggesting an ecosystem that was once warm and alive with a variety of life.

The fossil deposits were the result of bones having been buried under layers of mud beneath a river. "These rivers, many of which were broad," said Sereno, "buried the animals that lived along their margins—like dinosaurs—as well as animals that actually lived in the rivers, like the crocodiles, turtles, and fish."[6]

The fossil site provided clues about more than dinosaurs, crocodiles, and turtles. The team also discovered fossil evidence of such river animals as "small crabs, and the teeth, bones, and scales from many species of fish."[7] Somewhat unexpectedly, they also discovered the remains of a huge flying reptile, a pterosaur, with a wingspan of almost seven meters (twenty feet). One team member, Greg Wilson, occupied his time by looking for the tiniest fossils that are often overlooked when others are digging up dinosaurs. He found some extremely rare fossilized seeds that add to the picture of the types of plants that grew in the area once populated by dinosaurs.

One of the prize catches of the 2000 expedition was not a dinosaur, but the largest crocodile specimen ever found, called *Sarcosuchus* ("flesh crocodile").

The new specimen revealed that this creature could grow to become a twelve-meter (forty-foot) monster with a two-meter (five-foot) jaw. In addition to the huge skull, Sereno's team found limb bones and large, foot-long armor plates from the creature's back. This giant crocodile probably had a dinosaur for dinner from time to time.

Most of the skeleton of a long-necked, plant-eating dinosaur called *Nigersaurus* ("Niger lizard") was also recovered. This bizarre creature had a mouth packed with as many as six hundred slender teeth for plucking vegetation from branches.

In total, the 2000 expedition to Niger recovered five new predatory dinosaurs; five new plant-eating dinosaurs, including one with armor plating; six new crocodiles ranging in size from twelve meters (forty feet) to less than one meter (three feet); three new turtles; new fish and shelled **invertebrates** from the ancient riverbed; seeds; and mammal teeth.[8]

The bounty of fossils weighed eighteen metric tons (twenty tons). It was prepared for travel using 100 bags of plaster to make 274 **fossil jackets**—a protective wrapping created by applying burlap soaked in wet plaster to the outside of the specimen.[9] The wet strips are applied all over

The expedition team lies down behind the jaws of *Sarcosuchus* to mark out how big the crocodile would have been.

Sereno's team hoists a fossil protected by a burlap fossil jacket.

a fossil once it has been dug out. When the wrap hardens, it protects the bones from the bumpy ride back to the museum.

International fossil work brings with it a responsibility to the host country. Sereno's American team dug for fossils in Niger with permission from the Nigerian government. After Sereno's team in Chicago completed their study of the new specimens, they were returned to Niger for safekeeping and public display.

A Life With Dinosaurs

Despite his success, Sereno feels that there are many opportunities still awaiting young paleontologists who have the desire to hunt for dinosaurs. "There are plenty more dinosaur species to be described," claims Sereno. "We seem to be entering a Golden Era of sorts for new species, with six or seven new ones being described each year. That rate will probably slow down after another fifty years."[10] Even if that's true, it gives new paleontologists maybe three hundred or more new species to find and name.

Sereno encourages young people to find their hidden talent. "I think you can be whatever you want to be as long as you give yourself a chance," says Sereno. "Find the talents that are locked inside you.

PAUL SERENO

Occupation: Paleontologist and Professor

Title: Professor, University of Chicago; President and Co-Founder, Project Exploration Foundation; Explorer-in-Residence, National Geographic Society

Specialty: South American, African, and Chinese dinosaurs and their evolution

Education: Bachelor of Science (BS) in biological sciences, Northern Illinois University; Master of Arts (MA) in geological sciences, Columbia University; Master of Philosophy (MPhil) in geological sciences, Columbia University; Doctorate (PhD) in geological sciences, Columbia University

THE CARE AND TRANSPORT

Finding a fossil is one challenge. Carefully extracting it from the earth, protecting it, and transporting it back to a fossil lab for proper study is another challenge. Many experts are involved in preparing a fossil for display in a museum. The following are the basic steps required to make a fossil fit for study.

After the fossil of a large creature has been found in the earth, workers dig it up using a variety of tools. The work often begins with shovels and picks to remove big chunks of rock surrounding the fossil.

The location of the fossil is carefully recorded before removing it from the earth. This record helps scientists to piece together the puzzle of bones later. They also record the sizes of the bones and their relationship to other fossils in the area. They take many photos to remind themselves what the site looked like when they found the bones.

Rather than trying to pick out all of the bones right there on the spot, the fossil is usually removed as part of a larger chunk of rock. This big lump of rock can then be taken apart more carefully back at the fossil lab. Before the chunk of rock is removed, the parts of bones that are exposed are sprayed or painted with a special adhesive to protect them from being broken. Next, the fossil is covered with a thin layer of paper or aluminum foil. Finally, the entire block of rock and fossils is wrapped in a protective field jacket (also called a fossil jacket) made of burlap strips coated in wet plaster. Once hardened, the field jacket provides a hard shell that protects the fossil while it travels by air and land.

OF FOSSILS

To remove the chunk of rock, workers dig under and around it to pry it loose. If the chunk is too big to lift by hand, a hoist on a truck or even a helicopter can be used to lift the rock from the ground. The fossils are carefully packed in crates, labeled, and then transported back to the fossil lab.

In the fossil lab, the plaster field jacket is carefully cut open with a power saw. The plaster jacket is slowly pried off and the layer of paper or foil removed to expose the fossils.

The work of removing fossil bone from the rock is done slowly and with great care. Small power tools that chisel or hammer away small bits of rock at a time are useful for removing most of the rock.

When most of the rock has been safely removed, the fossil preparator switches to finer hand tools to remove the last bits of rock that are in contact with the fossil bones. Small hand tools such as chisels, dental picks, scrapers, and brushes are handy for these tasks. This work is sometimes very slow so that the bone is not damaged in any way.

A final step for removing fine pieces of rock from the bone is to use an air abrasion tool. This tool has a special nozzle that streams a very fine powder of baking soda, under pressure, onto the surface of the bone. The stream is powerful enough to remove tiny bits of rock without damaging the bone. Once the bone is clean it may still have small cracks in it. These are filled with a thin bead of epoxy cement to keep the bone strong and prevent cracks from spreading.

You can begin to do that by volunteering in labs and museums or by joining a group that is going into the field. In school, take lots of science—from math to biology—and also take art."[11] Sereno also has a realistic view of what you need to be a success at field-work in paleontology. Above all else, he says that you need lots of energy and very good legs for walking and working in the field.

To encourage aspiring paleontologists to find their hidden talents, Sereno has created the Project Exploration Foundation as a way of making science accessible to the public—especially minority youth and girls—through educational and field experiences with scientists. Project Exploration sponsors annual field trips for young people and families to dig fossils with Sereno and other paleontologists. On top of all of this, Sereno is also an Explorer-in-Residence with the National Geographic Society and continues his fieldwork in far-flung lands. His example is proof that a love of dinosaur science can enrich the lives of many people of all ages.

CHAPTER 5

Mysterious Dinosaurs of Madagascar

Some discoveries are a long time in the making. Such is the case with the dinosaurs of Madagascar, an island off the eastern coast of Africa. Much of the island is lush and green—not the typically dry and desolate badlands where dinosaur fossils are often found. The rain forest is populated by many unusual animals not found anywhere else in the world, including unusual species of lemurs, bats, foxes, and rodents. Fossils are found outside the jungles in a region that is much drier and lacks so much greenery, making it possible to dig into the ground without too much of a problem.

The first clues that dinosaurs once lived on Madagascar came in 1895. At that time, French paleontologist Charles Depéret found a few bones from a titanosaur—one of the giant, long-necked, plant-eating dinosaurs that were common in the southern hemisphere. The bones were few and unimpressive. They did not excite other scientists at the time.

Although French expeditions returned to the area several times, many of these early clues went neglected for nearly a hundred years. Then paleontologist David Krause from Stony Brook University in New York read Depéret's early report from Madagascar.

"I thought there was the potential for the discovery of more [fossil] material," recalled Krause.[1] After studying Depéret's report, he organized a series of return expeditions to Madagascar beginning in 1993 to search for fossils. Krause is most interested in mammal fossils. But he always brings several people who are interested in finding dinosaur bones on his

Palentologist Kristina Curry Rogers at a dinosaur exhibit at the Maryland Science Center

expeditions. Among the team he brought in 1998 was a young graduate student named Kristina Curry Rogers.

Some paleontologists wait a lifetime to make a big discovery. Only twenty-four at the time, Curry Rogers was about to experience the unexpected. She was brought along to help with the backbreaking work of digging up and packing worthy fossils found by the team. When she arrived at the fossil dig in Madagascar in 1998, it had already been partially worked for several years by Krause's earlier teams. Curry Rogers's hard work quickly turned into good fortune as she found herself in the middle of a major find.

"We dug into the hillside, and the more we dug, the more bones we found," said Curry Rogers. The scientists had found a remarkably complete skeleton of a titanosaur. Titanosaurs were among the last of the dinosaurs. Until the work of Curry Rogers and her colleague Catherine Forster, also from Stony Brook University, the fossil evidence for titanosaurs was spotty.

A Jumble of Bones

The titanosaur bones were found in a **bone bed,** a deposit in the earth of many disconnected bones. Bone beds are formed when one or more animals die and their body parts are swept into a common location by the current of a river or stream. Once trapped in the sand or mud, the bones become fossilized. A crook in a river is often a good collecting point for the bones of animals that may have died upstream. A bone bed may contain the parts of many different kinds of animals.

The good news about bone beds is that they contain a great wealth of fossils in a concentrated area. This makes it easier to locate all of the bones and dig them up. The bad news is that the bones are

A bone bed, like the one seen here, is a deposit of several fossil bones that were swept together by a river or stream.

jumbled together and disconnected, which makes an enormous jigsaw puzzle out of the remains.

Bone beds of dinosaurs also make for some heavy lifting. It is sometimes impractical to try to pick out all of the individual bones while still working in the field. Instead, fossil hunters carefully divide a bone bed into several smaller chunks of rock that can be removed individually. Each chunk is cut out of the rock using rock hammers, chisels, and pick axes.

The bones that Curry Rogers helped to dig up were packed in fossil jackets and shipped back to the United States for study. It was not until she began working on the bones in the fossil laboratory that she realized how important a discovery they had made. Included in the bone bed chunks were the parts of several titanosaurs, large and small. Among the bones were a nearly complete skeleton of a juvenile titanosaur and two nearly complete skulls.

"A specimen like this is incredible. You just don't expect to find something so amazing," said Curry Rogers. "Only a few of the tail bones were missing."[2]

Even though the skeleton was of a young titanosaur, not yet fully grown, the animal measured about eight meters (twenty-six feet) long.[3] A fully grown titanosaur would have been about twice as big as this specimen, perhaps fifteen meters (fifty feet) long and weighing about as much as two or three elephants.

The skulls of these juvenile titanosaur specimens provided scientists with the first complete picture of the titanosaur's head. The skull was small compared to the rest of the body and fixed on a long, slender neck. The skull had a narrow snout, but the nostrils were on top of the dinosaur's skull. This is quite different from the nostrils on most of today's familiar large mammals, such as rhinoceroses, tigers, and bears, whose nostrils are on the sides of the snout at the front of the skull.

The Curry Rogers titanosaur had a mouthful of peglike teeth. "Its teeth were okay for raking leaves off trees, but it couldn't crunch and wasn't a very efficient eater," explained Curry Rogers.[4]

Determining what kinds of plants this dinosaur ate was another challenge. The Madagascar fossil site did not provide any clues to the diet of this titanosaur. "Even though we've searched high and low, there just aren't a lot of plant fossils," Curry Rogers said. "The most interesting thing about its diet is that it lived—unlike other long-necked dinosaurs—after flowering plants had evolved. Maybe it dined on some of the first flowering plants! No matter what it was eating, it must've been eating pretty much all the time to maintain such high growth rates."[5]

Naming a New Dinosaur

Curry Rogers thought she may have found a new type of dinosaur. But before a new dinosaur can be named, a paleontologist must do extensive research to prove that he or she has actually discovered a new variety of dinosaur. This task was especially difficult for Curry Rogers, because titanosaur specimens—most being rather incomplete—are scattered across several continents.

"Since the first titanosaur was found a hundred years ago, we've had no idea of their anatomy," said Curry Rogers.[6] For two years, she traveled the globe to such faraway places as India, Argentina, and Russia to compare her dinosaur to those that had already been discovered.

After many months of study, Curry Rogers and Forster were finally certain that their dinosaur was a previously unknown member of the titanosaurs. They gave it the two-part scientific name *Rapetosaurus krausei*. What does the name mean?

Curry Rogers explains: "The Malagasy, or first people of Madagascar tell of a mischievous giant named Rapeto (ruh-PAY-too), kind of like our Paul Bunyan.

'Saurus' is Greek for lizard. And 'krausei' recognizes my colleague, David W. Krause, for his contributions to paleontology as well as to the health care and education of kids in Madagascar."[7]

Becoming a Paleontologist

Curry Rogers jokes about how long she went to college to earn her advanced degree in paleontology. Her love of dinosaurs led her to nine years of university education. Ironically, this passion for dinosaur fossils comes from a person who grew up in a state where such fossils were never found. "Where I grew up in southeast Missouri, the most common fossils I found were ancient marine creatures," explained Curry Rogers. "In fact, my first fossil loves were **trilobites**!" Her interest in science and fossils led to a fascination with dinosaurs as well.[8]

"I'm pretty sure that 'paleontology' was the first big word that I learned how to spell," admitted Curry Rogers. "By the age of six or seven I was already announcing my plans to be a paleontologist, though back then I thought that trilobites were the coolest things ever."[9]

Then came an opportunity to join a field trip. "I went on my first dinosaur dig as a girl scout at age sixteen, and knew that I'd be hooked forever!"[10]

Curry Rogers's lifelong education prepared her well for her career. Her broad knowledge of fossils has led to two interesting jobs that she maintains at the same time. As the Curator of Paleontology at the Science Museum of Minnesota, she not only works with dinosaur fossils but with other kinds of fossils, as well—"from clams to giant sloths." This job requires public appearances for the museum where she speaks to kids, parents, and teachers about dinosaurs. Her other job as a teacher at Macalester College introduces her love of fossils to new generations of aspiring paleontologists.

The Daily Job

The work of a paleontologist never seems to be done, even when you are not digging for fossils on an expedition. When she's not doing fieldwork, explains Curry Rogers, she is still "at work" at the museum where she does "a lot of writing and researching, usually on the dinosaurs that are my specialty (the long-necked sauropods), or on dinosaur growth rates."[11] Her busy schedule at the museum finds her working with visitors, even on the Internet where she goes online each week to answer kids' questions about dinosaurs and paleontology. She also puts her writing talent to good use as the author of a weekly column for the local newspaper about news in dinosaur science. As a professional scientist, she also attends different yearly meetings where researchers share their findings. Occasionally, she even helps museums design their exhibits by giving them advice about fossil creatures and their habitats. But that's not all.

Although she may have to work long hours, Kristina Curry Rogers loves her job. "Being a scientist is awesome!" she says.

NAMING DINOSAURS AND

A shark may simply be a shark to you, but *Carcharodon carcharias* is a particular kind of shark unlike any other. The name "shark" is the common name for this fish. The name *Carcharodon carcharias* is the scientific name for a particular species of shark: the great white shark.

A common name is useful for broad categories of things but does not necessarily help you tell the difference between one type of thing and another in the same category. For example, there are islands all over the planet, but there is only one island called Madagascar. Likewise, any kind of shark may be called a shark, but if a scientist wants to talk about a species of great white shark, he or she uses the scientific name *Carcharodon carcharias*. *Tyrannosaurus rex*, *Triceratops horridus*, and other Latin names given to dinosaurs are also scientific names.

Scientists around the world share a common set of rules for naming organisms and fossils. The scientist who first describes a species in a scientific publication is given the honor of naming it. The name is usually in Latin but may often include a "Latinized" version of a word from another language. All scientists use Latin for naming species so that scientists all over the world can use the same names. A French zoologist, for example, would use the same scientific name for a shark as a zoologist from China or any other country.

OTHER EXTINCT CREATURES

The scientific name of a species contains two words—the genus and species. The first, the genus, is the name of a bigger related group of similar creatures. The second, the species name, identifies an organism as being from a smaller group within the larger genus. For example, the genus *Carcharodon* includes both the great white shark and the megalodon shark. Only the great white shark has the species name *carcharias*.

A scientific name may also reveal something that makes the given species unique. It might be named after the place where it was found, the rock formation in which it was deposited, or something about its anatomy. In some cases, the name may tell us something about the imagined behavior of the fossil organism. This is the case of *Tyrannosaurus rex*, whose name means "tyrant lizard king," because scientists believe this large meat eater was a terror to other creatures. Once in a while, a scientist will honor a person by naming a species after him. But a scientist never names a species after herself, for to do so would be considered very bad manners!

KRISTINA CURRY ROGERS

Occupation: Paleontologist and Professor

Title: Assistant Professor of Vertebrate Paleontology at Macalester College; Curator of Paleontology at the Science Musem of Minnesota

Specialties: Paleoecology, the evolution of dinosaurs, and titanosaurs

Education: Bachelor of Science (BS) in biology, Montana State University; Master of Science (MS) in anatomical sciences, Stony Brook University; Doctorate (PhD) in anatomical sciences, Stony Brook University

"My job doesn't end at five P.M.," adds Curry Rogers, "or on weekends either—I do public speaking all over the country, at universities and colleges, for schools, libraries, and social groups."[12] Often, an accomplished paleontologist must be prepared to be in the public spotlight. This helps keep the public informed about new discoveries, sheds light on many of nature's mysteries, and encourages young people to form an interest in science.

Despite the long hours, Curry Rogers's enthusiasm for her work is boundless. "Being a scientist is awesome!" she exclaimed. "I love making discoveries, whether it is out in the field, in a museum collection, or even in a laboratory. There is so much left for us to learn about dinosaurs, and I love being a part of the process. . . . It's the search for answers that really excites me."[13]

CHAPTER 6

Fish With Legs:
Early Land Animals
From the Canadian Arctic

"We are lobe-finned fishes," declared paleontologist Ted Daeschler. He was speaking about human beings. The term *lobe-fin* refers to a kind of ancient fish that had four sturdy chest and hip fins with thick bones and strong muscles. "We are essentially very specialized fish. We have the same features as very primitive fish you find in the Devonian rocks."[1]

The Devonian Period is a geologic time span from long before the age of the dinosaurs. The early lobe-finned fishes to which Daeschler refers lived some 370 million years ago. To put that in perspective, the earliest humanlike mammals found in the fossil record date from only about 2 million years ago.

Daeschler is a scientist at the Academy of Natural Sciences in Philadelphia. His specialty is the **evolution** of the first land vertebrates. Vertebrates are animals with backbones, including fish, amphibians, reptiles, mammals, and birds. The first land vertebrates arose from fish living in freshwater streams and lakes. Daeschler links the evolution of humans to that of fish. The link has much to do with the four limbs found on most land vertebrates.

"[Humans] are just one of the animals that evolved from lobe-finned fishes," explained Daeschler. "We can trace our ancestry and the ancestry of all the other limbed animals back to that point 370 million years—or a little bit more—ago."[2]

Daeschler studies the history of the period in life when certain kinds of fish made the move to land. It is a time from which very few fossils are available. One of his recent discoveries, from the cold, harsh

Ted Daeschler poses with a fossil and model of *Tiktaalik*, one of the first fish to move to land.

climate of the Canadian Arctic, reveals much about this gap in our knowledge of vertebrate evolution.

A Quick History of Fish

The first life on the planet was in the oceans. The oceans were rich with oxygen and became home to the first vertebrates to evolve: fish. Fish adapted gills to draw oxygen out of the water. They also developed four strong fins for swimming. Fish were the first vertebrates to spread across the planet.

There are more kinds of fish than of any other vertebrate. The most varied fish belong to the group known as bony fish, whose skeletons are made of bone. This is the most ancient group of vertebrates with jaws, and it accounts for more than half of the living groups of vertebrates on land or sea. Bony fish lived as long as 416 million years ago.

The two major divisions of bony fish include the common ray-finned fish and the lobe-finned fish, which today are quite rare. There are more than 25,000 living species of ray-finned fish found in freshwater and saltwater habitats. The lobe-finned fish dwindled in numbers with the rise of the ray-finned fish, but not before some members of this group adapted into the first vertebrates to leave the water.

A key to their move to land was the sturdy nature of their strong, leglike front fins.

From Water to Land

By the late part of the Devonian Period, many of the lands bordering the oceans and lakes of the world had become green with tall land plants and seed ferns. The greening of the planet also enriched the air with oxygen, creating an inviting new world for animals to explore. A new variety of vertebrates, descended from the lobe-finned fish, began a cautious migration from the life-sustaining waters of their ancestors. They came out of the ooze and onto the rocks and mossy stretches of shoreline of the first habitable land. Thus marked a monumental event in the history of life, a transition that led to the first amphibians as well as all vertebrate lineages to follow, including reptiles, mammals, and birds.

Paleontologists such as Daeschler use the term *tetrapoda* to describe the first examples of land vertebrates and all of their descendents. A **tetrapod** is a vertebrate with four limbs that have fingers and toes. Strictly speaking, dogs, cats, dinosaurs, and even humans are all tetrapods descended from the first walking fish that left the water and took to life on land.

If, during the Devonian Period, the sea was so inviting and the land so bare of the necessities of life, why did some vertebrates venture onto land in the first place? This is one of the big questions that Daeschler has been trying to answer. While the fossil record of early fish is rich, there are few clues to the stage of evolution during which some lobe-finned fish took to the land. Such a creature would be half fish and half land animal. Daeschler focused his fieldwork on finding such a fossil. His hard work paid off in a big way in 2004.

How to Find the Fossil of a Walking Fish

Chance has little to do with finding early tetrapod fossils from the Late Devonian Period. There are only a few known places in the world where such fossils can be found, and most of these places are remote and hard to explore. Even when they can be found, fossils of such half fish, half land creatures are rare and mostly consist of only a few clues.

Many paleontologists hoping to find early tetrapods have returned to well-established fossil deposits, such as those in east Greenland, a cold country that is largely inside the Arctic Circle. A more risky and daring strategy is to find a site that has never included tetrapods before. Daeschler and colleague Neil Shubin took the latter approach and decided to explore a fossil location that was known for fish. What intrigued them was that the location may have represented a shallow-water habitat that early, transitional fish-tetrapods could have used.

Their strategy eventually paid off with the discovery of *Tiktaalik,* a lobe-finned fish that probably lived in the water but whose anatomical features would have allowed it to crawl onto land from time to time. The name *Tiktaalik* (tik-TAH-lik) was borrowed from the language of the local residents in the Canadian Arctic where the fossil was found. *Tiktaalik* is an Inuktikut word for a large, shallow-water fish.[3]

Finding *Tiktaalik*

The recognition of *Tiktaalik* was preceded by four years of exploring for fossils in the Canadian Arctic, where the summers are short and the sun shines for nearly twenty-four hours a day. The fossil site is located in a valley of the remote Ellesmere Island, about nine hundred seventy kilometers (six hundred miles) north of the Arctic Circle in Canada's Nunavut Territory. The site was known to contain fragmentary fish fossils from the Late Devonian Epoch.

The expeditions led by Daeschler and Shubin have each included between six and ten scientists and fossil collectors. Being in such a remote area meant that the site had not been picked over by too many people, giving hope that something new and significant could be found there. Although it is cold and barren, the location is almost ideal for collecting fossils because there is little vegetation to hide the tips of fossils weathering out of the rocks.

In 2000 some interesting fossil fragments found at the site gave the scientists hope that they might be on to something related to the evolution of tetrapods. Fossil evidence made it clear to them that the site once had a warm climate and consisted of a shallow-water environment close to land—an ideal habitat for the first tetrapods. Daeschler, Shubin, and various team members returned to the site several times, continuing their search until in 2004 they recovered several unusual specimens that turned out to be *Tiktaalik.* The fossils—still sealed in the rock—were wrapped in a plaster jacket by the team and then lifted by helicopter out of the remote arctic site. Once research was completed in the United States, the specimens were returned to a Canadian scientific institution for permanent keeping.

Even though the Canadian Arctic is a cold, harsh place, it is a good place to find fossils. Ted Daeschler and his team were able to spot fossils without any plants or trees getting in the way.

What the team found after studying the fossil-bearing rocks was startling. No less than three partial specimens of *Tiktaalik* eventually emerged as scientists in the laboratory carefully cleared away the rock from the bones. Nearly two years later, a clear picture of *Tiktaalik* took shape, and Daeschler and Shubin published the results of their discovery in 2006.

What *Tiktaalik* Tells Us

Tiktaalik filled an important gap in the fossil record of early land animals. The three specimens provided much information about most of the front half of the fish, including remarkably complete skulls, shoulder bones, and front fins—all preserved in their original positions. Two size ranges of *Tiktaalik* were found, the largest suggesting a body length of about three meters (nine feet).

Tiktaalik was clearly a fish with **adaptations** for staying out of the water for short periods of time. Its body and head were flat, with eyes on top, like those of crocodiles. Its nostrils were on the sides of its head, closer to the mouth, like other fish-tetrapods.

The fossils of *Tiktaalik* that Ted Daeschler and his team found help scientists understand more about how animals evolved.

Its ribs were longer than those of a fish, suggesting that *Tiktaalik* was somewhat capable of supporting its own weight out of the weightless medium of water. *Tiktaalik* also had a neck—a feature not seen in true fish, but essential for an animal that must lift its head out of the water to breathe air or to provide flexibility while walking on land. The skull included evidence of gills for breathing in water as well as structures that would have aided in sucking air without the gills, as in early amphibians.

The front limbs of *Tiktaalik* provided important clues to the transition of fish to tetrapods. They were short and finlike but had bones similar to those in the wrist of a land animal. The wrist design of *Tiktaalik* had similarities with bones that can still be seen in land animals today. Shubin explained that *Tiktaalik* "tells us to a great extent how parts of our own skeleton evolved."[4]

That was not *Tiktaalik*'s only claim to fame. The fossil specimen of *Tiktaalik* that Daeschler and Shubin found also showed the scientists that the transition from fish to tetrapod was taking place long before these animals left the water. Some extinct lobe-finned fish had limblike fins equipped with toes similar to those seen in tetrapods.

What did *Tiktaalik* look like in the wild? *Tiktaalik* probably resembled a cross between a large fish and a crocodile. It lurked in warm, shallow waters, raising its head up to look around and breathe air from time to time. *Tiktaalik* was a fish equipped with strong front legs and the ability to breathe underwater or outside of the water.

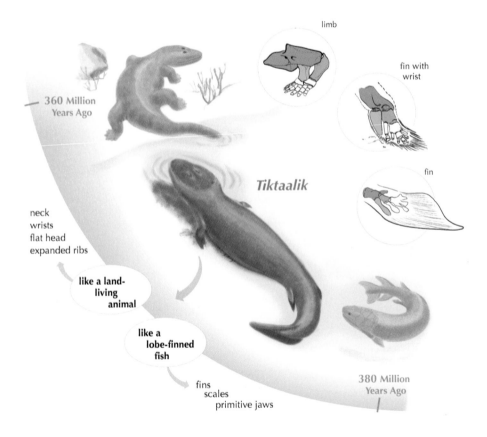

limb

fin with wrist

fin

360 Million Years Ago

Tiktaalik

neck
wrists
flat head
expanded ribs

like a land-living animal

like a lobe-finned fish

380 Million Years Ago

fins
scales
primitive jaws

Tiktaalik represents a stage in the evolution of some fish species to land-dwelling animals.

FISH OUT OF WATER:
THE EARLY TETRAPODS

Lobe-finned fish apparently evolved legs and lungs before they became land animals. These features probably helped them live in shallow-water environments. What would have driven some of them to eventually leave the water entirely?

Land represented a rich, uncharted new domain for animals that could breathe and move outside of the water. By the Late Devonian Period, saltwater and freshwater habitats were populated by an abundance of fish. Competition in the water was probably fierce. No matter how big a fish was, there was probably a bigger fish that could eat it. No such competition existed on land, where tetrapods found themselves to be the largest predators. Early tetrapods found a terrestrial world overflowing with a largely untapped source of prey in the form of terrestrial **arthropods**—insects, crabs, and spiders.

Although the first land vertebrates were not plant eaters, they benefited from the greening of the world by living in the safe shadows of plants, breathing the oxygen-rich air enriched by plants, and enjoying the lush, moist habitat that enabled them to effectively lurk for prey.

By the Middle Carboniferous Period, there is fossil evidence that insects had begun to eat plants. This development led to more and more insects and expanded the primary food source for tetrapods. By the Late Carboniferous Period, some vertebrates developed a taste for plants. This gave them a virtually unlimited new source of food.

Tetrapods left the water, therefore, to occupy a largely untapped habitat in which they were the biggest, baddest creatures around.

EDWARD B. "TED" DAESCHLER

Occupation: Paleontologist

Title: Associate Curator of Vertebrate Biology at the Academy of Natural Sciences in Philadelphia

Specialties: Early freshwater vertebrates and the nature of nonmarine ecosystems

Education: Doctorate (PhD) in paleontology, University of Pennsylvania

"Here's a creature that has a fin that can do push-ups," said Shubin. "This is clearly an animal that is able to support itself on the ground." While on land, *Tiktaalik* probably waddled like a seal.[5] Like crocodiles and seals, *Tiktaalik* was also a meat eater. Its primary food source was probably other fish.

"It might have pulled itself onto stream banks, perhaps moving from one wet area to another, and even crawled across logs in swamps," added Daeschler.

Daeschler and Shubin continue to return to their remote fossil site in the Canadian Arctic to try to find more clues about life from the Late Devonian

Period, when the line between fish and land animals was blurred.

What is perhaps most amazing about their discovery is that it tells us some important things about the evolution of animals that eventually led to humans. "Ancient fish bones," writes Shubin, "can be a path to knowledge about who we are and how we got that way." The bones of *Tiktaalik* contain early versions of skeletal structures of the neck, head, and limbs that eventually transformed into the skeletal features of people. This ancient fish captures the fascination and mystery that surrounds the discovery of fossils but also means so much more. Fossils not only reveal the secrets of long extinct animals, they form a link between the deep past and the present.

The study of fossils—the science of paleontology—is closely connected to living things that exist today. Through the study of fossils, we can examine the ways in which life of the past adapted to the changing world, providing clues to the great detective story of human existence and ways in which people are more or less equipped to deal with their own world in transformation.

CHAPTER 7

Plan Ahead!
How to Prepare for a Career in Paleontology

There is no single path to a career in paleontology. The six scientists profiled in this book are proof of that. Each came to the study of extinct life in his or her own unique way. Some became interested in dinosaurs while they were still young children. Others only became interested in fossils later in life, even after college.

Even though they took different paths to careers in paleontology, these individuals share many talents and interests. They are curious about nature and the world around them. They are careful thinkers who enjoy solving problems and puzzles—true fossil "detectives." For field work, they have the patience needed to detect and dig up the fragile bones of extinct creatures. For those times when they work behind desks or with the public, these scientists share an ability to communicate well with written and spoken words. This enables them not only to explain their ideas to other scientists but also to make complex ideas understandable for students, parents, and teachers. Finally, each of these people has a commitment to the education of others, sparking an interest in paleontology that might inspire a beginning scientist.

If you happen to be one of those lucky people who have these skills, there could be a bright future for you in the study of fossils. Here are some tips that will help you plan a career in paleontology.

Education

By the time many young people reach high school, dinosaurs already seem like kids' stuff. One reason for this is that keeping up with science is hard work, even for a kid. Science classes in middle school and high school rarely spend much time on the subject of dinosaurs—there are just too many other things in this world to learn about.

If you are truly interested in paleontology, however, you can begin to take steps while in middle school and high school to prepare for a career as a dinosaur hunter. Paleontology combines knowledge from many different kinds of science and math. Take courses in geology, biology, and physics to give you some background in the natural world of earth science and living things. Math and computer science are also important to paleontology.

It is a good idea for aspiring paleontologists to continue to improve their writing and speaking skills. Take English composition classes, or even take a class in public speaking. Knowledge of a foreign language is also helpful in the wide world of science, as you may encounter many colleagues from other countries. In the course of your career you will also encounter scientific papers written in other languages, so any background in European or even Asian languages would be helpful. Perhaps above all else, getting good grades in high school is key to getting into the college of your choice.

CAREERS IN PALEONTOLOGY

Most people with degrees in paleontology are not actually doing fossil work for a living. One of the leading professional associations in the United States dedicated to paleontology only has about 1,500 members. Most of these are either graduate students or teachers of biology and anatomy at the college level. Fossils themselves are rare and require much time to dig up and prepare, a factor that limits the field of jobs to those who are most dedicated. Many paleontologists are able to do their fossil work part of the time while they handle other jobs, such as teaching. Like with many of the paleontologists profiled in this book, being a paleontologist often combines several jobs into one: hunting for fossils, working in a museum, teaching college, and writing books, to name a few.

Nobody gets rich working as a paleontologist, but you can earn a decent living. Annual salaries range from about $35,000 for a junior paleontologist at a museum to over $50,000 if you become the chief curator or scientist in your organization. Teaching jobs, especially at the college level, provide better salaries at the largest institutions, where professors may earn an annual wage of $100,000 or more.

Here are just a few of the kinds of jobs that you may wish to explore as a paleontologist:

College professor—Paleontology professors obviously do much of their work with fossils, but even geology and biology professors may also have the opportunity to do some fossil field work as part of the job.

Museum curator—Museum curators are the people in charge of exhibits. A curator of fossils gets to manage a museum's fossil collection and exhibits.

Government geologist—Geologists map geologic formations and identify mineral resources for the government. They are sometimes asked to help on fossil digs or other work related to paleontology.

Paleo-artist—There is much work available in the illustration of scientific articles as well as educational books about fossils, dinosaurs, and other extinct creatures. Knowledge of paleontology gives an artist a terrific advantage in this work.

Writer or journalist—Some lucky people have been able to make a living writing about dinosaurs and other prehistoric creatures. Books, magazines, and news stories are produced every day to keep the public informed about new discoveries and theories in paleontology.

Another good way to get some experience in natural science is to take a volunteer job at a local museum. You may even be able to go on field trips with local scientists who need the help of young people to dig up fossils. These experiences will give you a better idea whether a career in paleontology is right for you. Volunteer experience can also be a big help in getting into a good college or university.

Most paleontologists continue on to college and graduate school. Whatever your chosen focus in paleontology, try to find a university or graduate program that specializes in what interests you most. There are many choices. Professors at these schools are happy to write to or speak with prospective students, even if they are still attending high school. Some of the brightest high school science students are offered scholarships to universities with wonderful paleontology programs.

Other Paths to Paleontology

There are many more opportunities for a career in paleontology than there used to be. Digging for fossils is just one aspect of being a paleontologist. Even more work is done back in the laboratory, where fossils are studied, theories are formed, and paleontologists contribute to an understanding of how life evolves and eventually becomes extinct. Paleontology embraces many different kinds of study and science.

As Kristina Curry Rogers says, "This is a great time to be a budding paleontologist. Paleontology has always been a field that borrows methods and tools from other fields to answer . . . questions. Right now, there is such a boom in the . . . methods [that paleontologists use] that there are a million new questions to be answered. Now, get to it!"[1]

Chapter Notes

Chapter 1. Dinosaurs of the Mongolian Desert

1. Perle Altangerel, M.A. Norell, L.M. Chiappe, and J.M. Clark, "Flightless Bird From the Cretaceous of Mongolia," *Nature*, vol. 362, 1993, pp. 623–628.

2. Mark A. Norell, J.M. Clark, Luis M. Chiappe, and D. Dashzeveg, "A Nesting Dinosaur," *Nature*, vol. 378, 1995, pp. 774–776.

3. Mark A. Norell, J.M. Clark, D. Demberelyin, B. Rinchen, Luis M. Chiappe, A.R. Davidson, M.C. McKenna, P. Altangerel, and Michael J. Novacek, "A Theropod Dinosaur Embryo and the Affinities of the Flaming Cliffs Dinosaur Eggs," *Science*, vol. 266, 1994, pp. 779–782.

4. Ji Qiang, Philip J. Currie, Mark A. Norell, and Ji Shu-An, "Two Feathered Dinosaurs From Northeastern China," *Nature*, vol. 393, 1998, pp. 753–761.

5. American Museum of Natural History, "An Interview with Mark Norell," n.d., <http://www.amnh.org/exhibitions/dinosaurs/interviews/transcript_norell.php> (April 28, 2009).

6. Roy Chapman Andrews, *Under a Lucky Star* (New York: Viking, 1943), p. 50.

7. Mark A. Norell, "A History in the Desert," *American Museum of Natural History*, n.d., <http://www.amnh.org/exhibitions/expeditions/gobi/history.html> (December 2, 2008).

8. Michael Novacek, *Dinosaurs of the Flaming Cliffs* (New York: Doubleday/Anchor Books, 1996), p. 227.

9. Ibid., p. 17.

10. American Museum of Natural History, "Mark Norell," *Seminars on Science*, 2006, <http://www.amnh.org/learn/welcomecenter/profiles/mnorell.php> (April 28, 2009).

11. Mike Novacek and Mark A. Norell, "July 11, 1998," *Dispatches: Dinosaurs in the Desert,* July 11, 1998, <http://www.amnh.org/exhibitions/expeditions/gobi/dis711.html> (April 28, 2009).

12. Ibid.

13. Thomas R. Holtz Jr., *Dinosaurs* (New York: Random House, 2007), p. 283.

14. Ibid.

15. American Museum of Natural History, "Mark Norell."

16. American Museum of Natural History, "An Interview with Mark Norell."

17. Edward Summer, "An Exclusive Interview with Dinosaur Detective Mark A. Norell, Co-Discoverer of *Mononychus*," *The Dinosaur Interplanetary Gazette*, 1993, <http://www.dinosaur.org/bznorell.htm> (April 28, 2009).

18. American Museum of Natural History, "An Interview with Mark Norell."

Chapter 2. Dinosaurs at the Bottom of the World

1. Thomas H. Rich and Patricia Vickers-Rich, *Dinosaurs of Darkness* (Crows Nest, New South Wales, Australia: Allen & Unwin, 2000).

2. Museum Victoria, "Victoria's Dinosaurs," *Prehistoric Life*, n.d., <http://museumvictoria.com.au/prehistoric/fossils/vicdinos.html> (November 25, 2008).

3. Thomas R. Holtz Jr., *Dinosaurs* (New York: Random House, 2007), p. 249.

4. Ibid.

5. Society of Vertebrate Paleontology, "Patricia Vickers-Rich," *PaleoProfiles*, 2007, <http://www.vertpaleo.org/education/profiles/prich.cfm> (November 25, 2008).

6. Ibid.

7. Ibid.

8. Ibid.

Chapter 3. Giant Dinosaurs From Argentina

1. BBC, "Extreme Dinosaurs," *BBC.co.uk*, November 23, 2000, <http://www.bbc.co.uk/science/horizon/2000/extremedino_transcript.shtml> (November 25, 2008).

2. Wayne Grady, *The Bone Museum* (New York: Four Walls Eight Windows, 2000), p. 107.

3. Ibid., p. 108.

4. BBC.

5. Luis M. Chiappe, "First Dinosaur Embryos Found with Fossilized Skin," *American Museum of Natural History*, 1998, <http://www.amnh.org/exhibitions/expeditions/dinosaur/patagonia/index.html> (April 29, 2009).

6. Luis M. Chiappe and Lowell Dingus, *Walking on Eggs* (New York: Scribner, 2001), p. 173.

7. Personal interview with Rodolfo Coria.

8. BBC.

9. Ibid.

10. Malcolm Ritter, "Huge Meat-Eating Dinosaurs Roamed in Groups in Argentina, Scientists Say," *Associated Press*, April 17, 2006, <http://www.usatoday.com/tech/science/discoveries/2006-04-17-big-dinosaur_x.htm?POE=TECISVA> (November 25, 2008).

Chapter 4. Lost Dinosaurs of Africa

1. Steve Brusatte, "Profile: A Portrait of Dr. Paul Sereno," *Australopithecus*, n.d., <http://sasap.freeservers.com/australopethicus/profile.html> (April 29, 2009).

2. Paul Sereno, "Two Predatory Dinosaurs Unearthed in Morocco," May 13, 1996, <http://www-news.uchicago.edu/releases/96/960513.dinosaur.shtml> (November 25, 2008).

3. Paul Sereno, "Niger, 1990," *Project Exploration*, n.d., <http://www.projectexploration.org/n_1990.htm> (November 25, 2008).

4. Ibid.

5. Gabrielle Lyon, "Dinosaur Expedition 2000," *Project Exploration*, n.d., <http://www.projectexploration.org/niger2000/11_28_2000.htm> (November 25, 2008).

6. Ibid.

7. Ibid.

8. Ibid.

9. Ibid.

10. Michelle Laliberte, "Tracking the Dinosauria Family Tree: An Interview with Dino Hunter Paul Sereno," *Odyssey Magazine,* September 2000, <http://www.accessmylibrary.com/coms2/summary_0286-28271620_ITM> (April 29, 2009).

11. Ibid.

Chapter 5. Mysterious Dinosaurs of Madagascar

1. D.L. Parsell, "Skeleton of New Dinosaur 'Titan' Found in Madagascar," *National Geographic News,* August 1, 2001, <http://news.nationalgeographic.com/news/2001/08/0801_madagascardino.html> (November 25, 2008).

2. Ibid.

3. Kristina Curry Rogers and Catherine A. Forster, "The Last of the Dinosaur Titans: A New Sauropod From Madagascar," *Nature,* vol. 412, August 2, 2001, pp. 530–534.

4. Parsell.

5. Science Museum of Minnesota, "Questions for Kristi Curry Rogers: Archive," 2004–2009, <http://dev.smm.org/buzz/museum/ask/rogers/questions_archive> (April 29, 2009).

6. Ibid.

7. Ibid.

8. Ibid.

9. Society of Vertebrate Paleontology, "Kristi Curry Rogers," *PaleoProfiles,* 2007, <http://www.vertpaleo.org/education/profiles/kcurryrogers.cfm> (April 29, 2009).

10. Science Museum of Minnesota.

11. Society of Vertebrate Paleontology.

12. Ibid.

13. Science Museum of Minnesota.

Chapter 6. Fish With Legs: Early Land Animals From the Canadian Arctic

1. Neil Shubin and Ted Daeschler, "How Fish Came Ashore," WGBH, *Evolution Library*, n.d., <http://www.pbs.org/wgbh/ evolution/library/04/3/text_pop/l_043_41.html> (November 25, 2008).

2. Ibid.

3. Edward B. Daeschler, Neil H. Shubin, and Farish A. Jenkins Jr., "A Devonian Tetrapod-Like Fish and the Evolution of the Tetrapod Body Plan," *Nature*, vol. 440, April 6, 2006, pp. 757– 763.

4. Chris Smith, "Interview With Neil Shubin," *Nature Podcast*, April 6, 2006, <http://www.nature.com/nature/podcast/v440/ n7085/nature-2006-04-06.html> (November 25, 2008).

5. Malcolm Ritter, "Fossil Fish Sheds Light on Transition," *Associated Press*, August 5, 2006, <http://www.boston.com/ news/science/articles/2006/04/05/fossil_fish_sheds_light_on_ transition/?p1=MEWell_Pos4> (November 25, 2008).

Chapter 7. Plan Ahead! How To Prepare for a Career in Paleontology

1. Society of Vertebrate Paleontology, "Kristi Curry Rogers," *PaleoProfiles*, 2007, <http://www.vertpaleo.org/education/ profiles/kcurryrogers.cfm> (April 29, 2009).

Glossary

adaptations—Responses made by a living thing to changes in its environment.

arthropods—A group of animals without backbones that have segmented bodies and a jointed exoskeleton. Arthropods include trilobites, crabs, lobsters, brine shrimp, barnacles, insects, spiders, scorpions, and centipedes.

curator—A museum worker in charge of a collection of valuable things, such as a collection of dinosaur fossils.

dig—A place where fossils are dug up; to dig up fossils.

dinosaur ("terrible lizard")—A group of land-dwelling reptiles that lived millions of years ago and had an upright body posture supported by two or four legs; birds are the only living descendants of dinosaurs.

ecosystem—The interrelationship of living organisms and the environment in which they live.

evolution—The natural process that causes species to gradually change over time, controlled by changes to the genetic code—the DNA—of organisms.

extinct—The dying off of an entire group or species of plant or animal.

forelimbs—The two front limbs (arms, legs, wings, fins, and so forth) of an animal.

fossil—Any physical trace of prehistoric life.

fossil jacket—A protective wrap made of burlap and soaked in plaster, used to protect a fossil bone.

invertebrate—An animal without a backbone.

overburden—Rock that lies on top of a fossil, which must be removed to access the fossil.

paleontologist—A scientist who studies prehistoric life, often using fossils.

predator—An animal that actively seeks and feeds on other live animals.

scavenger—An animal that feeds on the remains of dead animals.

sedimentary rock—Mud, sand, and other materials deposited over time and eventually turned into rock; sedimentary rock may contain fossils.

species—In classification, the most basic biological unit of living organisms; members of a species can mate and produce offspring.

tetrapod—Vertebrate animals with four legs as well as two-legged and legless vertebrates descended from them. This group includes amphibians, reptiles, mammals, and birds.

trilobite—An extinct family of marine invertebrates related to the spider.

vertebrae—One of the bones that makes up the spine, or backbone.

vertebrate—An animal that has a backbone.

Further Reading

Books

Dingus, Lowell, Luis M. Chiappe, and Rodolfo Coria. *Dinosaur Eggs Discovered!: Unscrambling the Clues.* Minneapolis: Twenty-First Century Books, 2008.

Hall, Kelly Milner. *The Random House Dinosaur Travel Guide.* New York: Random House, 2006.

Larson, Peter, and Kristin Donnan. *Bones Rock! Everything You Need to Know to Be a Paleontologist.* Montpelier, Vt.: Invisible Cities Press, 2004.

Malam, John, and John Woodward. *Dinosaur Atlas.* New York: DK Publishing, 2006.

Norell, Mark. *Unearthing the Dragon: The Great Feathered Dinosaur Discovery.* New York: Pi Press, 2005.

Internet Addresses

Walking With Dinosaurs: Australian Dinosaurs

<http://www.abc.net.au/dinosaurs/meet_the_dinos/ozdino1.htm#2>

Fighting Dinosaurs
(American Museum of Natural History)

<http://www.amnh.org/ology/paleontology/fightingdinos/index.html>

Project Exploration

<http://www.projectexploration.org/>

Index

N

names, common *vs.* scientific, 92–93
National Geographic Society, 77, 80
navigation, 69
Niger, 64–76
Nigersaurus, 74
Norell, Mark, 9, 14–17, 19, 21, 25–28
Novacek, Michael, 15

O

Osborn, Henry Fairfield, 12
overburden, 55
Oviraptor, 9

P

paleontologists, 4–5
paleontology, 4, 7, 11–12, 25–28, 110, 113–115
Patagonia, 45–46, 50–52, 62
polar regions, 29–30, 40–42
Project Exploration Foundation, 80
Protoceratops, 23–25
pterosaurs, 73
public speaking, 90, 94, 113

R

Rapetosaurus krausei, 84–89
Rich, Thomas, 30, 32, 35–40, 42
risks, 19, 56, 69

S

Sahara Desert, 68–71
salaries, 114
Salgado, Leonardo, 51
Sarcosuchus, 73–74

Science Museum of Minnesota, 90
seeds, 73
Sereno, Paul, 64–80
sharks, 92–93
Shubin, Neil, 102–110
species names, 93
Suchomimus, 70
sun exposure, 56

T

taxonomy, 92–93
teaching, 32, 44, 64, 67, 90–94, 114, 115
tetrapods, 100, 108
Tiktaalik, 101–110
titanosaurs, 59, 83–89
training. *See* education.
travel benefits, 11–12, 63, 64, 88
tyrannosaurs, 52
Tyrannosaurus rex, 64, 92, 93

U

Ukhaa Tolgod, 16–17
University of Chicago, 64, 66

V

vehicles, 20
Velociraptor, 23–25
vertebrates, 97
Vickers-Rich, Patricia, 30–32, 35–44
volunteering, 26–27, 48, 80, 89–90, 113–116

W

weather issues, 19–21, 35–36, 53–56, 71
Wilson, Greg, 73